PRAY TO WIN!

Prayers for Successful Spiritual Warfare

_____

by Tracey L. Smith

Obey My voice, and I will be your God,
and you shall be My people.
And walk in all the ways that I have commanded you,
that it may be well with you.
Jeremiah 7:23

~~~

Follow Jesus.

Matthew 4:19

Whoever you choose to follow on earth... whether Jesus or Satan... is
who you will follow into eternity. Unfollow Satan. ***Follow Jesus!***
~Tracey L. Smith

~~~

About the Cover

~~~

The cover of this book features a warrior suited with the whole armor of God *(Ephesians 6:13-17)*. The kneeling warrior has defeated many enemies in the name and by the power of Jesus Christ. The humble warrior is now bowed in submission to God. He is prepared for peace but also ready for the next victorious battle against enemies that oppose the advancement of God's Kingdom.

Be strong in the Lord and in the power of His might. Put on the whole armor of God so that you can successfully stand against all the devil's methods of attack.

For our fight is not against any physical enemy: it is against organizations and powers that are spiritual.

We are up against the unseen power that controls this dark world and spiritual agents from the very headquarters of evil. Therefore, you must wear the whole armor of God so that you may be able to resist evil... and even when you have fought to a standstill, you may still stand your ground.

Take your stand then with truth as your belt, righteousness as your breastplate, the Gospel of peace firmly on your feet, salvation as your helmet, and in your hand—the sword of the Spirit, [which is] the Word of God. Above all, be sure you take faith as your shield, for it can quench every burning missile the enemy hurls at you.

[Also] Pray at all times with every kind of spiritual prayer, keeping alert and persistent as you pray for all of Christ's men and women.

Ephesians 6:10-18 (J.B. Phillips New Testament)

Dedication

~~~

This book is lovingly dedicated to my three God-fearing,
Holy Spirit-filled children: Matthew, Joshua, and Hannah Smith.
Your love, prayers, and excellent behavior through homelessness and the
countless trials we faced as a family kept me going when I wanted to
give up. I thank God for you all and love you with all my heart.
May God continue to bless you.
May He continue using you to share the love of Jesus with others.
You are beacons of His holy light.

~~

To my beloved mother, the late Eloise Finney Redding.
Your light still beams through those you left behind.
You were a shining example of motherhood, strength, and of God's love.
You gave LOVE a good name!
You are sorely missed and still very much loved and admired.
Thank you for pointing me to Christ. I love you always.

~~

To my heroic father, Charles Redding.
You demonstrated how to stand strong amidst violent storms.
You fought fierce battles with odds against you and won!
You did it with grace and made courage look easy.
Your family is stronger because of you.
I love you and bless you.

Table of Contents

Introduction

~~~

At age eleven, a few weeks after being hit by a car, I wrote my first prayer. Looking back, I probably should have prayed before I nabbed a can of pork and beans from the local store, darted across a busy street, and got hit by a car in the first place... but I digress.

Nevertheless, at a young age, I learned two valuable lessons: 1) crime doesn't pay, and 2) God is ever-present and merciful. God was with me as I lay injured in the street. A doctor driving down the street witnessed the accident. He attended to me as I went in and out of consciousness. He helped me until the ambulance came and took me away. I believe that it was not a coincidence that the doctor was present when I was hit by the car. In my opinion, it was God who ordered his steps to be there at that precise moment.

The First Inspired Prayer

One day, a few weeks after I was hit by the car, my mother was in the kitchen cooking. I wanted to be close to her, so I sat at the kitchen table to write a poem. Writing was something I loved doing. At a certain point, I noticed a cloud surrounding me. The cloud brought words to my mind, which formed a prayer—a prayer that was an answer to a prayer.

You see, each night at bedtime, my mother made my siblings and me kneel at our bedsides to recite our prayers. We learned the *"Now-I-lay-me-down-to-sleep"* prayer. However, the part that says, *"If I should die before I wake ..."* didn't sit right with me, so I wouldn't say it. Mom asked me about it, and I shared how it bothered me, so she tried teaching me *"The Lord's Prayer."* That was also a no-go. It was too long, and I would forget the words.

Feeling frustrated, I prayed to the Lord for my own bedtime prayer, and He answered me. God gave me a prayer from the cloud—a cloud that only I could see in that kitchen—a cloud that was actually the Holy Spirit.

At age eleven, I called my first inspired prayer *"The Family Blessing Prayer."* It went like this:

Bless thy mother.

Bless thy house.

Bless thy children and thy spouse.

Bless thy father and thy kin.

Forgive us, Lord, for all our sins.

Glory to God! Although I didn't know what the word "spouse" meant, I finally had my own nightly prayer. It was easy to remember and did not mention dying. I shared it with my mother, explaining about the cloud and how words came to my mind when the cloud was present. Mom was very encouraging to me. She also explained what the word "spouse" meant. *(Smile)*

Two years later, my dear Christian mother passed away, but her encouragement remained. For decades, I have been inspired by the Holy Spirit to write.

The prayers in this book are composed to help Believers experience continuous victories. They are an answer to my prayers for help to defeat an enemy who pummeled me in times past—but no more!

As you pray, remember, *"Greater is He that is in You, than he that is in the world."* (1 John 4:4)

Take courage, take faith, and know that Jesus is with you in warfare. Be sure to thank God and give Him glory for all your victories. Then kneel humbly as the warrior on the cover, in your divine armor, ready for your next assignment to defend against the enemies of God.

How to Use This Book

~~~

In today's complex world, Believers are faced with the challenge of navigating serious spiritual threats along with evading the allures of sinful temptations and treacherous entanglements. Witchcraft and Satanism are on the rise, and deception is at an all-time high, making it more difficult to stay on the right path. We need the Lord's help.

The prayers in this book offer understanding and strategic, tactical insights tailored for both new and seasoned Christians to engage safely in spiritual warfare to try and remain on the right path. Readers can use their God-given authority to triumph over the enemy and secure victories over spiritual threats through faith in Christ Jesus.

IMPORTANT: To benefit from the prayers within this book, you must be born again. This means you have accepted Jesus Christ as your Lord and Savior and have, therefore, made a wise choice to be on the Lord's side in the ongoing battle of good vs. evil. For this choice, you may rejoice to know that:

- Only those on the Lord's side are equipped with the armor of God for spiritual protection. *(Ephesians 6:11-17)*
- Only those on the Lord's side have been given power and authority over all the power of the enemy. *(Luke 10:19)*
- Only those on the Lord's side are more than conquerors through Christ Jesus. *(Romans 8:37)*

FACTS: Only those who have accepted Jesus Christ as Lord and Savior *(born-again Christians)* are on the Lord's side *(Romans 10:9-10)*.

Spiritual warfare is absolutely necessary to live victoriously as a Christian and enjoy the abundant life Jesus promised *(John 10:10)*. Those who choose to do nothing about enemy attacks forfeit their own victories and peace. Essentially, they live in defeat by their own choosing, often because they haven't been taught how to fight in the spirit with their words. Prayerfully, that will change.

(Unsure if you are a Christian? Please pray the "Salvation Prayer" in this book.)

Spiritual Warfare Combinations

While most of the prayers in this book are self-explanatory, below are examples of prayer combinations that have proven successful.

Issue(s)	Recommended Warfare Prayers
Recurring workplace issues	• *Pray both of the "Workplace" prayers* • *Prayer to Break Curses* • *Protection from Witchcraft and Evil*
You or your family are under attack or face multiple issues *Note: You don't have to pray all of the prescribed prayers on the same day. You may choose 2 or 3 one day, and 2 or 3 the next day. Then repeat that cycle for a couple of weeks or until you see results.*	• *"Prayer to Break Generational Curses" or "Mercy Prayer to Lift a Curse" (if generational curses have already been broken)* • *Prayer to Break Curses* • *Protection from Witchcraft and Evil* • *The Lord's Prayer* • *Isaiah 41 Covering Prayer*
You have recurring troubling dreams or dreams of snakes, eroticism, weapons directed at you, or others.	• *Recite the prayer that corresponds with your dream(s)* • *Psalm 64 Protection Prayer* • *Prayer to Break Curses* • *Prayer to Break Unholy Covenants*
You dream about the deceased	• *Quickly pray the "Prayer After Dreams About the Deceased"* • *Prayer to Break Generational Curses*

Note: Unless otherwise specified, prepare to recite/pray each prescribed prayer three or more times per week for at least two weeks. This is warfare. Put in the work (3-5 minutes/day). Fight for your best life in Christ!

Two prayers are particularly beneficial if they are prayed immediately:

- Prayer After a Dream with Food
- Prayer Against the Enemy and Avenger

Prayer After a Dream with Food. If you have a dream where you see or eat food, please pray the *"Prayer after a Dream with Food"* as soon as you wake up, if possible, to prevent or at least minimize sickness, disease, or other issues. The enemy may use food *(unholy catering)* to plant sickness or disease in your body or set up unholy covenants to gain legal access to your life. Expel the unholy food(s) and break the unholy covenants right away.

Prayer Against the Enemy and Avenger. Pray this soon after you receive a blessing, a breakthrough, or after you perform a good deed. Have you ever heard the saying, "No good deed goes unpunished?" That's partly true because of the enemy and the avenger. They are foul spirits bent on punishing those who **do good or receive good**. They want to discourage and punish good behavior and dampen the joy received from rewards and breakthroughs. Refer to *"Who Are the Enemy and Avenger?"* to learn more.

Q&A

Should I fast before praying spiritual warfare prayers?

Fasting is a good idea but is not mandatory for most of the warfare prayers. It's entirely up to you. However, fasting is encouraged before praying the following prayers: *"Generational Curse Prayer," "Mercy Prayer to Lift a Curse," "Prayer to Break/Cut Soul Ties,"* and possibly the *"Prayer against Lust and Masturbation."*

Be responsible. You know your body and medications. You may opt to do a shorter fast or just fast one particular food item. Your fast doesn't have to be days or weeks long. Use your best judgment. Talk to your pastor. Consult your physician if needed.

Do I need to open doors or windows to let demons escape?

No. You do not need to open doors or windows to let demons escape. They are spiritual beings that can enter and exit through walls, windows, and other physical matter.

Do I need to burn sage, crush a red brick, or drop salt?

No. You will not be required to burn sage, crush a red brick *(to break curses),* or drop salt or cayenne pepper in or around your house to drive demons away. The power of Jesus is more than sufficient.

Other Things to Know About This Book

Words in italics. These are optional words to add to your prayer *(if applicable).* Example: I pray for my job, relationships, ***family, marriage, children,*** health, wealth, etc. The ***italicized*** words are optional.

Repeat 2x. This is a suggestion to repeat the verbiage two times.

What is the abyss? *(Pronounced "uh-biss")* When you cast out demons and tell them to go away, Luke 11:24 tells us that the demons go to dry, parched places, also known as the abyss. *(Also see Luke 8:30-31 NKJV).* Note: They hate the abyss.

Repetitive Scriptures. Most of the warfare Scriptures in this book are repeated throughout. This is by design to build the faith needed for successful spiritual warfare. You've got to believe and be able to stand on God's word. Romans 10:17 says:

So, then faith comes by hearing, and hearing by the word of God.

How the Author Uses This Book

~~~

Truthfully speaking.

My most common spiritual battles are with occult workers who attack my loved ones, myself, or others whom I am committed to serving. If there are indicators that evil or witchcraft is afoot *(i.e., recurring or unusual troubles, confusion, brain fog, unrest, dreams identified in this book, depression, loss of willpower, loss of energy, destiny derailment, job troubles, business or ministry troubles, etc.);* then I will pick one or two of the protection prayers and pray each one **three or more times a week for at least two weeks.** *(The two I most often pray are the "Protection from Witchcraft and Evil" prayer and the "Psalm 64 Protection Prayer.")* I might also throw in the *Prayer to Break Curses* on one or two of those days each week as well. The end goal is to block and stop demonic attacks. If you wait too long before engaging in spiritual warfare *(reciting warfare prayers),* you may have to put out more fires or bigger fires.

Now, I know that unrepented sin can diminish or delay results, so I repent daily. I also read the Bible and try to live in accordance with God's commands.

Regularly, I ask the Lord to reveal if there is anyone I have not forgiven. If someone pops into my mind, I simply say, *"I choose to forgive (name). Please help me, Holy Spirit."* God will give grace while the process of forgiveness runs its course. It may take a while, in some cases, but repeat daily, *"I choose to forgive (name)"* until forgiveness is realized. Unforgiveness is a heavy burden. I choose to take Jesus' yoke upon myself, for His yoke is easy, and His burden is light. *(Matthew 11:30)*

I get attacked in my dreams, too. Through dreams, the enemy tries to connect and form a covenant to gain legal entry into our lives to wreak havoc.

If I have a dream about a snake, for instance, I will pray the *"Prayer After a Dream with Snakes"* three or more times a week for at least two weeks. I might also pray the *"Prayer to Break Curses"* on one or two of those days and also throw in the *"Protection from Witchcraft and Evil"* prayer two days a week for two weeks.

The last example I'll share pertains to unholy covenants. The enemy uses many tactics (including dreams) to form alliances with us, so I pray the *"Prayer to Break Unholy Covenants"* regularly—like once a week—to keep the enemy at bay.

Repetition is Powerful

~~~

To repeat, or not to repeat—that is the question.

Repetition is powerful. We learn our A-B-Cs through repetition. We learn new skills through repetition. We get up and report to work repeatedly. We recite and repeat Scriptures to commit them to memory. The sun and moon rise and set on repetitive cycles. Doctors prescribe medicine to be taken repetitively for best results. So, yes, repetition is powerful, and it works, particularly in spiritual warfare.

There are some who believe that repeating prayers should be avoided, rationalizing that God heard them the first time and there's no need to repeat prayers. However, the Parable of the Persistent Widow challenges that rationale. In Luke 18:1-8, Jesus shared the parable of a widow who made repeated requests for justice against her adversary. In the end, her persistent, **repetitious** requests paid off, and she received the desired justice. Jesus concluded the parable by saying:

Will not God bring about justice for His chosen ones who cry out to Him day and night? Will He keep putting them off? I tell you; He will see that they get justice, and quickly. Luke 18:7-8 (NIV)

In addition to the parable, I can share from years of experience that there are no penalties for reading, re-reading, repeating, or reciting prayers, especially warfare prayers.

Repetition, persistence, and consistency produce results.

Did you know that many in the occult read and repeat incantations, hexes, and spells from books? They understand the power of words and the power of repetition. Moreover, because their efforts produce the desired results, they are motivated to continue their evil deeds.

We, as children of Light, should be wiser than those who walk in darkness. Our power through Christ is greater than theirs. *(1 John 4:4)*

With just a mustard seed of faith, we can override all the evil that is sent our way by using words—words that are read, recited, or prayed **repeatedly.** Repetition is powerful.

Walk uprightly.

Walking uprightly cannot be overstated. I want to shout it from the highest rooftop with a king-sized megaphone. The breastplate of righteousness is part of the armor of God. Righteousness and holiness matter and practicing them pleases God. If you live unrighteously, you run a high risk of reopening the very doors and portals that were closed through your spiritual warfare efforts. Now, if that happens, just repent. Ask the Lord to help you make any necessary changes, and then take up your armor and re-engage in spiritual warfare to drive the enemy away again. Never give up. Fight for your best life in Christ!

God is with you in warfare.

In the Old Testament Scriptures, God's people faced many physical enemies. **The Lord was with them in battle**—but battle they did! They took up their own physical weapons and fought. The Lord did not grab their swords and shields and take up hand-to-hand combat with their enemies. No! God's people had to take courage and faith and go into battle, fighting in the name of God repeatedly.

The struggle continues.

God's people still face many enemies today. **The Lord is with us in battle**—but battle we must! We must take up our own weapons— spiritual weapons—and wrestle against spiritual enemies. *For we wrestle not against flesh and blood... (See Ephesians 6:12).* Just like in days of old, the Lord will not take up our weapons and engage in spiritual warfare against our enemies. He gave us the power and weapons to engage successfully. He will back us, but we must take courage and faith and fight in the name of Jesus, repeatedly.

Never surrender!

You must strike repetitive blows to defeat the enemy. The enemy might be gone after that first week of spiritual warfare; however, you should continue your assault by repeating your warfare prayers for another week *(a total of two weeks)* to stomp out any remaining embers. **Do not have mercy on demons.**

Again, when engaging in spiritual warfare, repeat your prayers several times a week for <u>at least</u> two weeks. This will also train you in what to say when you don't have this book in your hand. Repeat until they retreat.

Regular pest control.

You may find it necessary to repeat the same process several times a year. It's like treating a home for insects. You treat it, but then you have to re-treat it, or the pests will come back. Demonic forces are the same. They are pests. You can drive them away with warfare prayers, but you may have to repeat the prayers again and again to keep the enemy at bay. **Welcome to spiritual warfare.** This is the life of a Christian warrior. We must be aware of what's going on in the spirit and then bravely take action to stop it.

Repeat warfare prayers as often as needed. Do not let the enemy infest your life and run amuck. Do not let him destroy you and those you love and care about.

Have no fear. Jesus is near, and it's not too late to start fighting for your best life in Christ!

God Wants You to Win

~~~

God is for you and wants you to win your spiritual battles!
Your victory brings glory to His Kingdom.

God's people are not meant to be defeated. You have a family in heaven that is cheering for you! God, Jesus, the Holy Spirit, and the entire host of heaven are fans of yours. They are cheering for you to win your spiritual battles. The Lord Jesus gave you indestructible, divine armor plus power over all the power of the enemy. **You have the advantage.** You can and should bring home the win for your team.

Too often, the enemy's team gets to stroll away in victory, elated that they have defeated, and in some cases, utterly destroyed, a superior opponent—a Christian. It doesn't have to be this way. Your defeat does not bring glory to the Kingdom of God. **God wants you to win.** So, why are Christians losing battles that they can easily win? The Lord says:

*My people are destroyed for lack of knowledge **AND BECAUSE THEY REJECT KNOWLEDGE.** Hosea 4:6*

The Lord Jesus walked the face of this earth demonstrating how to live sin-free, fearless, and abounding in miracles. He showed us how humankind was created to live. He demonstrated that all things are possible through God when He walked on water, raised the dead, fed the 5,000, and performed many other miracles. He demonstrated the ability to live in this world as a chosen people of God without succumbing to a life of debauchery, greed, idolatry, and unholiness. He also demonstrated that we have power over demons, but we like to dismiss that. *"Oh, no! That's spooky,"* some would say. Others might hide behind: *"I try not to think about the enemy. I don't give place to him."* That's not true. Often, those same people give place to the enemy by cussing, lying, stealing, lusting, gossiping, fornicating, envying, committing adultery, watching porn, worshipping idols *(people and/or carved images)*, visiting palm readers, using tarot cards, or a host of other sins too numerous to name here. However, when it comes to praying and strategizing to defeat an enemy who is using those same vices to destroy them—they take the *"I-don't-give-place"* position.

The truth is there's a lack of knowledge. The truth is those who walk in defeat may not fully understand or believe that they inherited victory when they accepted Jesus Christ as Lord and became part of God's holy family. Hopefully, the information in this book will help to change that. God wants us all to bring home the "WIN" and emerge victorious over every spiritual battle.

Once you identify where the battles are *(in the mind, home, family, finances, health, job, business, general spiritual warfare, generational curses, etc.),* you can engage in spiritual warfare and defeat the enemy by using your words. You can pray to win.

Heaven is cheering for you! Be brave. God wants you to win!

> *What then shall we say to these things?*
> *If God is for us, who can be against us?*
> *Romans 8:31*

Why Pray if God Knows Everything?

~~~

At its core, the primary purpose of prayer is to spend time with God. God already knows what you need before you ask. He truly is all-knowing. Nevertheless, prayer was established for you to slow down, humble down, and come talk to Him. He wants a relationship with you.

When you spend time with God in prayer by talking with Him from your mouth or heart, you cultivate a relationship with Him.

He already knows what you'll ask, and what His answer will be, but as your Father, He desires your presence. He wants to spend time with you and impart spiritual and/or physical blessings into your life.

Your relationship with God will grow when you pray.

So, *"Why pray if God knows everything?"*

The answer is to spend time cultivating and developing your relationship with Him. That's why you should always pray.

Spiritual Warfare

~~~

Spiritual warfare is an ongoing battle between good and evil. Spiritual warfare is Biblically based. It is not a mere metaphor but a real, ongoing, mortal battle between two kingdoms: the kingdom of darkness and The Kingdom of Light. All of humanity is part of this battle, and human souls are the prize. The origin of this battle is detailed below.

War in Heaven

Michael (the Archangel) and his angels fought against the dragon (Satan), and the dragon fought and his angels and prevailed not; neither was their place found any more in heaven. (Revelation 12:7-8)

And the great dragon was cast out, that old serpent, called the devil (Satan), which deceives the whole world: he was cast out into the earth, and his angels were cast out with him. (Revelation 12:9)

So, the devil and his army fought against Michael and the angels of God. Satan's gang lost the battle and were kicked out of heaven.

Jesus said, ***"I beheld Satan as lightning fall from heaven."*** *(Luke 10:18)*

War on Earth

After his lightning-fast expulsion from heaven, Satan landed on earth, and he was angry. Revelation 12:12-17 records the following:

Woe to the earth and the sea because the devil has come down to you with great fury because he knows his time is short.

And when the devil saw that he was cast unto the earth, he persecuted the woman, Israel, because from Israel, the man child— the Savior of all humanity—Jesus Christ, came forth.

Then, the dragon was enraged at the woman and went off to wage war against the rest of her offspring—those who keep God's commands and hold onto their testimony about Jesus.

To this day, the forces of darkness wage war against humanity, particularly those who keep the commandments of God and those who follow Jesus. The others are already under Satan's control and following him to eternal damnation. Yet, they, too, will suffer on earth and then again in hell if they don't repent. The devil hates all of humanity. The only hope is to accept and follow Jesus.

Humanity's Role in This Epic Battle

Be alert! Be on watch! For your enemy, the devil, roams around like a roaring lion, looking for someone to devour (1 Peter 5:8 GNT).

Put on the whole armor of God and give no place to the devil, neither in words nor actions. Do not consider lofty opinions, knowledge, or arguments raised against *(i.e., challenging)* the knowledge of God. Rather, capture every thought and make it obedient to Christ. *(See Ephesians 6:11, Ephesians 4:27, 2 Corinthians 10:5)*

For the weapons of your warfare are not carnal *(physical)*, but mighty through God to the pulling down of strongholds *(2 Corinthians 10:4)*. Use your authority. You have been given authority and power over all the powers of darkness, and nothing shall by any means hurt you, nor shall any weapons formed against you prosper. *(See Luke 10:19, Isaiah 54:17)*

Spiritual warfare is real and necessary in this current age. Fight for your best life in Christ, knowing that God is with you, and **He wants you to win!**

Take a Stand

~~~

Jesus Has Your Back

One of my favorite movies is *"The Bear" (c. 1988. IMDb tt0095800).* The film narrates the story of an orphaned bear cub that embarks on a solitary journey across the wilderness, having numerous adventures and mishaps. Eventually, the cub meets Big Bear *(a type of savior)* and begins to follow him, much like we should follow Lord Jesus. Big Bear is mature and adept at navigating obstacles. He knows the way. He knows how to overcome.

Toward the end of the movie, a mountain lion begins pursuing the little bear to devour him. Instinctively, the cub tried to escape the merciless predator by running away. The little bear ran and ran, but the lion was hot on his trail. I was pulling for the cub. I wanted him to be safe, but alas, the cunning predator caught up to Little Bear and took a swipe at him, slashing him and drawing blood. The precious little cub hardly had a chance. He had run as far as he could and was now backed into a corner under attack by a deadly enemy seeking his life. At that moment, Little Bear, who was now injured and face-to-face with his enemy, did something surprising... **He took a stand!**

With as much strength and fervor as he could muster, the cub roared at the lion! He was likely saying, "GO AWAY! LEAVE ME ALONE!"

Then there was another surprise... The mountain lion stopped right in its tracks, turned around, and went away! Yes! The enemy stopped its attack and let the courageous little bear cub live!

What caused the enemy, the mountain lion, to retreat?

Was it a sudden feeling of compassion or mercy for the cub? Nah... That beast had no mercy.

Did the lion suddenly become fearful of the cub who took a stand? Nope... That beast was a seasoned predator and destroyer.

The truth is that the mountain lion was not afraid of Little Bear at all. He knew he had the advantage of years and experience over the little bear, and he was also more powerful.

So, what REALLY caused the enemy to retreat?

Well, standing several feet behind the cub was Big Bear. Yep, the same adult bear who had been watching over the cub throughout the movie. When Big Bear saw the cub take a stand against his enemy, Big Bear backed him. Big Bear stood up and roared at the lion in unison with the cub. **The cub had a mighty force standing behind him, literally**—a force that could defeat and end that lion quickly—and the lion knew it. That's why the enemy retreated! He saw who was backing the cub.

It's a powerful scene—my favorite—because I imagine the Lord Jesus backing us when we take a stand against the enemy. In the same way that the little bear took a stand, so can we.

We are soldiers with supernatural weapons and armor. Jesus did not leave us here defenseless to be bullied and devoured. We can only be defeated if we refuse to use our weapons. As Christian soldiers, we must not run. We must stand up for ourselves, and the enemy will retreat. He knows that those who follow Jesus have been given power over all the power of the enemy. He knows that we have the most powerful One backing us ... Jesus! Jesus can defeat the enemy in less than a millisecond. The Lord will never leave us nor forsake us. He is with us to enforce mercy. He will make the enemy retreat so we can live. When we roar, Jesus roars with us!

Take courage! Take faith! Take a stand!

Command the enemy to stop and leave you and yours alone, knowing that King Jesus has your back! You can pray to win!

Fight or Flee?

~~~

What should you do when you're under enemy attack?

The Holy Spirit taught me to deal with demons head-on! He taught me to **flee** from the appearance of evil and **flee** from sin and idolatry—but He taught me to **fight** against *(resist)* evil.

He used the example of a hornet's nest attached to a house. Should the nest be left there to grow and get stronger? Absolutely not! That nest has to come down! The sooner, the better. It presents a danger that must not be ignored.

Likewise, demonic forces present danger that must not be ignored. The weapons of our warfare are not carnal *(physical)*, but spiritual. We have the power to cast down enemy forces with our words. We can resist the devil by casting down thoughts that do not align with the word of God.

When engaging in spiritual warfare, remember that we fight against demonic forces. We do not fight against or curse people. God loves everyone—saved and unsaved. Let the Lord deal with the people.

Remember, vengeance is the Lord's. He will repay. You may rest assured that every person will reap what they have sown, whether good or evil. Ask the Lord to help you forgive your enemies and walk in love. This pleases the Lord, and it is healthy for your soul.

> ***For our struggle is not against flesh and blood but against the rulers, against the authorities, against the powers of this dark world, and against the spiritual forces of evil in the heavenly realms. (Ephesians 6:12)***

James 4:7, 1 Thessalonians 5:22, 1 Corinthians 10:14, 2 Corinthians 10:5, Ephesians 6:12

How Witchcraft Works

...and how it can be defeated

~~~

Ye are of God, little children, and have overcome them: because greater is He that is in you, than he that is in the world. (1 John 4:4)

Jesus defeated all the power of the enemy, including witchcraft, and He gave us, His followers, the power to do the same. Jesus said:

Behold, I give unto you power to tread on serpents and scorpions, and over all the power of the enemy: and nothing shall by any means hurt you. (Luke 10:19)

When we pray, the Lord hears us, and if He wills, He will dispatch angels to manifest our prayers. If our prayer does not align with God's will or is out of sync with His timing, it may not be manifested, or it may be delayed until the appointed time. In either case, we must rejoice because we have an audience with The Most High through Jesus Christ, our Savior and High Priest. Whether or not any specific prayer is answered, we must remain faithful to God.

Consider the passage below from Daniel 10:12-13 (NIV). An angel appeared to Daniel and spoke these words:

Do not be afraid, Daniel. Since the first day that you prayed, your words were heard, and I have come in response to them. But the prince of the Persian kingdom resisted me twenty-one days. Then Michael, one of the chief princes [of God], came to help me because I was detained there with the king of Persia[1].

This passage supports the fact that prayers are heard and answered by God. It also reveals that spiritual battles can delay the manifestation of answered prayers.

How witchcraft works.

When occult workers *(witches, sorcerers, etc.)* conjure, chant, curse, raise demonic altars, or otherwise direct evil toward others, demonic forces are mobilized *(instead of angels)* to make those words manifest.

I will go ahead and say it...

Witches are not magical people with special powers. They are hell-bound servants of Satan who are connected to and in covenant with demons and familiar spirits that carry out their evil curses and spells.

To be clear, the witches are not able to execute their own witchcraft; instead, familiar spirits *(familiars)* and demons enforce the witchcraft and sorcery they practice. Those same demons, spirit guides, and familiars will, for certain, turn on them one day, and they *(the witches and occult workers)* will be dragged off into the darkest corners of hell to be tormented for eternity unless they repent.

How to defeat witchcraft.

As a Christian, you have the power to win against witchcraft because **greater is He (Jesus) who is in you than he who is in the world (Satan).** *1 John 4:4*

Now is the time for more Christians to learn how to defend against witchcraft and enemy attacks. We must have spiritual situational awareness. That is to say, we must know when we are under attack. Then, we should not bury our heads in the sand or run away. Instead, we should engage in spiritual warfare to protect ourselves and those we love.

Use the protection prayers in this book to block and stop witchcraft. They have been tested and proven to work for many others. Have no fear. Pray to win!

[1] A strong man *(i.e., Ruler, power, or principality referred to in Ephesians 6:12)*

Casting out Demons

~~~

Many people deny the existence of demons and evil spirits. This denial is, unfortunately, a victory for Satan. It allows Satan and his armies to wreak havoc without challenge, expulsion, and without so much as an acknowledgment of their evil presence. Those who refuse to believe in evil spirits do two things:

1. They make themselves easy targets for the enemy, a merciless predator whose primary goal is to steal, kill, and destroy.

2. They unwittingly call Jesus a liar because Jesus cast out demons! Before Jesus, no one was casting out demons on command like that! His contemporaries marveled. Jesus was, and still is, a phenomenon! Our Savior turned the world right side up!

Demons are real, and we, as followers of Christ, have the power to drive them away. Consider this example set by our Lord, Jesus Christ:

*[Jesus] arose … and He entered a house and wanted no one to know it, but He could not be hidden. **For a woman whose young daughter had an unclean spirit [a demon]** heard about Him, and she came and fell at His feet.*

*The woman was a Greek by birth, and she kept asking Him to **cast the demon out** of her daughter. But Jesus said to her, "Let the children [the Jews] be filled first, for it is not good to take the children's bread and throw it to the little dogs."*

And she answered and said to Him, "Yes, Lord, yet even the little dogs [non-Jews] under the table eat from the children's crumbs."

*Then He said to her, "For this saying, go your way; **the demon has gone out of your daughter."***

*And when she had come to her house, she found **the demon** gone out, and her daughter lying on the bed. Mark 7:24-30*

In another account, the Lord cast out impure spirits *(demons)* from the man at the tombs:

*[Jesus and His disciples] went across the lake… When Jesus got out of the boat, a man with an **impure spirit** came from the tombs to meet Him. This man lived in the tombs, and no one could bind him anymore, not even with a chain. No one was strong enough to subdue him. Night and day among the tombs and in the hills, he would cry out and cut himself.*

*When he saw Jesus from a distance, he ran and fell on his knees in front of Him. He shouted at the top of his voice, "What do you want with me, Jesus, Son of The Most High God? In God's name, don't torture me!" For Jesus had said to him, **"Come out of this man, you impure spirit!"***

Then Jesus asked him, "What is your name?"

*"My name is Legion," he replied, "for we are many." And he begged Jesus not to order them to **go into the abyss** (Luke 8:31 NIV).*

*A large herd of pigs was feeding on the nearby hillside. The demons begged Jesus, "Send us among the pigs; allow us to go into them." He gave them permission, and **the impure spirits came out** and went into the pigs. The herd, about two thousand in number, rushed down the steep bank into the lake and were drowned.*

Those tending the pigs ran off and reported this in the town and countryside, and the people went out to see what had happened. When they came to Jesus, they saw the man who had been possessed by the legion of demons, sitting there, dressed and in his right mind; and they were afraid. Those who had seen it told

*the people what had happened to the demon-possessed man—and
told about the pigs as well. (Mark 5:1-16)*

If you believe in the Bible, then after reading these accounts, there
should be no doubt about the existence of demons and no doubt about
Jesus' authority over them... authority that He gave to us. *(Luke 10:19)*

True Story

Once upon a time, I met a Christian lady who was heavily burdened
with troubles and convinced that she bore a curse. As a result, she had
become depressed and hopeless. She needed help, and I was ready to
serve. While she spoke about her many problems, I sought the Lord, in
my heart, for guidance on what He would have me do for her.

He provided guidance, and I was ready to serve by breaking any
curses spoken against her by humans, but she wanted none of that. She
believed she was a good person and hadn't done anything wrong, so
there couldn't possibly be demons around her. As for the curse she
believed was plaguing her, she had a remedy. Her pastor had anointed
her head with oil, and the lady thought that would fix everything.

"Wow!" I thought. For decades, the Holy Spirit has been training me
and others in spiritual warfare, and you mean to tell me all we ever
needed was a vial of anointing oil? ... ***Wrong!!***

I was happy that she had faith, but sad she was trusting in an
incomplete remedy. I asked more questions and learned that she had
been anointed with oil months earlier and had seen no improvements in
her life. I knew something was amiss because it shouldn't take that long
to begin seeing results. With effective spiritual warfare, improvements
should be realized, on some level, in 90 days or less, and it was way past
90 days. She stated that she was waiting on the Lord. ***What??*** I had to
hold my tongue as I stood there, sent by the Lord, willing and able to
help. Her wait could have been over, but she rejected it.

God had come through for her. He had sent someone with compassion to help, but she rejected it. Pride, ignorance, or something else kept her from accepting that demons were indeed affecting her life, and they needed to be cast out. Anointing oil, alone, had not fixed her problems—nor would it ever. I wanted to help, but God's word is true:

*My people are destroyed for lack of knowledge **AND because they reject knowledge**. Hosea 4:6*

I ran into that beloved sister months later, and unfortunately, there was no change. She continued to rely on anointing oil. Can you see how God wants to help, but we can tie His hands with unbelief, rejection, or lack of knowledge? It's not fair to blame God for our self-defeat.

Throughout the Old Testament, the Israelites took up their weapons to defend against their adversaries:

- Samson took the jawbone of a donkey and went to battle, defeating a thousand enemies by himself. *(Judges 15:15-17)*
- David used a stone and slingshot to battle and defeat the giant, Goliath, in the name of God. *(1 Samuel 17:48–50)*
- And there were others... BUT

Not one of them went into battle swinging a vial of oil.

Anointing oil is good and holy and has its purpose—I carry a vial of it; but we need more than anointing oil to break curses, subdue witchcraft, and stop the enemy from destroying us! We need to use our words and faith to manifest those victories.

We must put on the whole armor of God to cast out demons and defeat the enemy. *(Ephesians 6:11-17)*

Indestructible Weapon of Praise

~~~

Once upon a time, there was a demon in my house. It was a sinister, stubborn demon. **The hair on the back of my neck stood up** when I drew near to confront it. For hours, I quoted Scriptures and shouted, *"I bind you, demon! I command you to get out, in the name of Jesus!"*

No matter how much I shouted commands and quoted Scriptures, that thing wouldn't budge. After many hours, its stubbornness began to wear me down. I began to doubt the word of God, questioning myself, *"Do I really have power over all the power of the enemy, as the word of God says?" (Luke 10:19)* It was then, that I realized the trick of the enemy was to make me doubt God's word. He had pulled the same "doubt-God-trick" on Eve in the Garden of Eden. With that realization, I felt righteous indignation rise from within, and I became more determined to win. Instead of waning, my faith in God's word grew stronger, and I fiercely resolved to defeat the ungodly, invisible force standing there, challenging me in my own home.

My energy was recharged, and I continued a barrage of commands, including Scriptures, until finally, after about four hours, the evil spirit departed, and the peace in my home was restored. However, I was left exhausted and nursing a sore throat.

After that long and difficult battle, I sought wisdom from the Holy Spirit, asking if there was anything I could have done differently. That level of effort was not sustainable or repeatable for the amount of warfare that I regularly faced.

The answer didn't come right then, but eventually I was taught about the power of praise and its effectiveness in spiritual warfare. I learned that praise is an efficient way to cast out even the most stubborn demons, and also principalities. Neither can withstand the power of Godly praise and worship, even if you're singing or playing praise and worship at a low volume.

From then on, I've never spent hours casting out evil forces. I just bind them, command them to go, and then break out in praise and worship or play praise and worship songs. No more exhaustion and no more sore throats. I learned to cast out demons with the indestructible weapon of praise.

The Fray in the Hallway

One evening, I was braiding my 14-year-old daughter's hair. We were chatting and bonding when we heard what sounded like two very heavy feet drop—one foot at a time—into the upstairs hallway. *Boom! Boom!* Startled, my young daughter ran and crouched on the side of the bed to hide. Incensed that someone would be in my home—and be loud and bold about it—I was compelled to go and see what was going on out there.

I started down the hallway but stopped abruptly due to an overwhelming evil presence. It caused the hairs on my arms to stand up. That's when I realized the loud, bold intruder was a demon—not a person! I discerned that it was very big, bigger than the one I had encountered years ago in a different home and city. The demon seemed to be hulking and towering over me. Fear tried to grip me, but I resisted. I knew this was no ordinary demon but something greater. It was a strongman.*

Whenever I have to face off with the devil himself or with rulers, authorities, and principalities *(i.e., strongmen)*; I rebuke them in the name of the Lord. I do not bind and send these higher demonic powers into the abyss. They will not move. So, I stood there with full confidence that the greater One was in me and shouted, *"The Lord rebukes you. Get out of this house!"* Then, I began to sing a praise song; the song *"Hallelujah!... Lord, we love You... Lord, we praise You... etc."* to be exact.

I sang a few rounds and then I felt a warm presence by my side. It was my young daughter. She had come out from hiding to stand with me and join the fray in the hallway. I was so proud of her courage and faith. We sang together, and within seconds, the evil presence was gone. The hair on my arms lay flat again. Peace was restored. My daughter's faith was increased, too. I was not exhausted, and my throat was not sore.

Thank the Lord! I didn't have to spend hours fighting. We really do have power over all the power of the enemy, just as Jesus said. We need only pick up our weapons and use them. The weapons of our warfare include righteousness, truth, faith, salvation, peace, the *(spoken)* word of God, praise, fasting, prayer, and power from Jesus over all the power of the enemy.

Remember, God is with you, and He wants you to win. You can defeat the enemy with the weapons of your warfare and the undefeated, indestructible weapon of praise. To God be the glory!

*Strongmen are also known as principalities, powers, rulers, authorities, and princes. They are fallen angels that are more powerful than demons. They dwell in the heavens and take pleasure opposing God's will. Michael, the Archangel, and others take them down. (See Daniel 10:11-13, Revelation 12:7-10.) Praise will always drive the unholy beings away.

When needed, I ask Father God, in the name of Jesus, to send angels to remove strongmen, as you will see in some of the prayers within this book. As humans, we cannot command angels, for we are lower than them (Psalm 8:4-5). Angels are under God's command (Psalm 91:11), but we can request their help through God.

Simple Commands to Cast out Demons

~~~

Below are simple, quick, and effective commands to bind and cast out unholy spirits from a habitation or a person. Pray with authority, faith, and courage. Jesus Christ will back you, and the demons <u>will</u> go away. Remember, Jesus said:

> *Behold, I give you authority to trample on serpents and scorpions and over all the power of the enemy, and nothing shall by any means hurt you. (Luke 10:19)*

(Cast out demons from yourself (me) or another person (name))

By the power of Jesus Christ, I command every demon that is harassing, influencing, or affecting *(name)* in any way to release *(name)* right now! I bind all demons and send them into the abyss.

I break all unholy covenants that have been made knowingly or unknowingly by *(name)*. I plead the blood of Jesus and put up a hedge of protection around *(name)*. All demonic attacks against *(name)* are blocked and stopped right now, in the mighty name of Jesus. Amen.

(Cast out demons from a habitation)

By the power of Jesus Christ, I bind and send to the abyss every demon in this *(home, church, office, basement, room, etc.)*. You are commanded to leave right now, in the mighty name of Jesus.

(Follow up with praise and/or worship when possible.)

Who Are the Enemy and Avenger?

~~~

Out of the mouth of babies and infants,
You have established strength because of Your foes,
*to still the **enemy** and the **avenger**.*
Psalm 8:2 (ESV)

The enemy and the avenger are Satan's minions. They are revengeful spirits who seek to punish and retaliate against those who do good and those who receive blessings. These evil spirits are foes and adversaries of both God and man. The enemy and avenger can appear at any moment to discourage you, challenge your faith, put stumbling blocks in your way, cause trouble, or block your progress through a variety of circumstances, distractions, issues, and calamities.

I have noticed that these foes tend to strike more frequently after a positive event, such as a breakthrough or a blessing, has been received.

Therefore, it is wise to safeguard yourself after performing a good deed or immediately following a breakthrough, blessing, promotion, or other achievement. The enemy and the avenger will attempt to use people and demonic forces to cause trouble, setbacks, discouragement, and anything else to dampen your spirits and rain on your parade.

The *"Prayer against the Enemy and Avenger"* is inspired to still *(stop)* the enemy and the avenger. Repeat the prayer often—three or more times a week, for at least two weeks after your blessing, breakthrough, or good deed. Fight for your best life in Christ! Pray and protect yourself from the enemy and the avenger.

(More on page 11)

Prayer Against the Enemy and Avenger

~~~

Dear heavenly Father,

I acknowledge Your sovereignty and submit to Your authority. No other people are so blessed to have their god near them the way You, Lord God, are near us. (Deuteronomy 4:7)

Lord, I confess my sins and ask for Your forgiveness.

In the name of Jesus Christ, I bind and send to the abyss the enemy, the avenger, and all evil spirits that are near me, watching me, monitoring me, affecting me, speaking against me, or planning to attack me, or my livelihood, my home, vehicle, *family,* relationships, and anything that I own, rent, borrow, or oversee. *(Repeat 2x)*

- I bind and send to the abyss all evil forces and demons sent to block, hinder, torment, harass, frustrate, distract, steal, kill, and destroy me.
- I bind and send to the abyss all demonic spirits connecting me to people who steer me away from God and His righteousness or stifle my progress, growth, and blessings.

I plead the blood of Jesus and ask You, Lord, to put up a hedge of protection around me and overthrow all rulers, powers, and authorities in the heavens that oppose my spiritual growth, favor, breakthroughs, and blessings.

Lord, You are the source of my peace, protection, and prosperity. You make my future secure. My destiny rests in Your merciful, kind, and loving hands. I am grateful, Father, for all that You have done and will do for me. In Jesus' name, I pray. Amen.

Psalm 8:2, Deuteronomy 4:7, Psalm 16:5 (NET)

Unholy Covenants

~~~

Establishing an unholy covenant is one of the ways the enemy gains access into our lives.

A few years back, I attended an office meeting. Virtual meetings were not yet popular. Although six people were invited, only two of us showed up—me and a woman who had obtained notoriety for leading a large prayer group.

Though we had just met for the first time, we quickly discovered a common interest… talking about the goodness of the Lord! It's funny how Christians often seem to find and connect with each other about the Lord.

While waiting for others to join the meeting, we continued to share and bear witness to our faith. Eventually, she confided in me about something personal. She shared that she was being physically attacked by a demon while she slept. She had prayed for the attacks to stop, but they continued. One morning, she awakened to find scratches on her body that were so deep she had to call out of work for several days.

She didn't know why she was being attacked or why she was being led to share her issue with me, but I knew. As an apostle, the Lord has equipped me to help His people in spiritual warfare and deliverance.

Nevertheless, after her confession, there was a brief pause between us as I sought the Lord's guidance to help her. She broke the silence by asking, *"Is there a word from the Lord?"* Immediately, the Holy Spirit told me to ask her if she had ever been involved in the occult.*

Thankfully, the prayer warrior was honest and humble. She confessed to attending séances and experimenting with Ouija boards as a teen. As a consequence of those activities, she had unknowingly entered into an unholy covenant with the devil. That's where he gained permission to attack her physically. Unholy covenants open portals that allow demonic entities to enter and disrupt lives or physically touch us.

We all make mistakes, and no one is perfect, so there was no judgment. I led her in a prayer to repent, renounce, and break any unholy covenants she entered. It went something like this:

> *Lord God, I repent for dabbling in the occult. I renounce my involvement with Ouija boards, séances, and any other occult activities. I break all unholy covenants and agreements that I made with the devil, and I close all portals to the enemy forever.*
>
> *I now reclaim any blessings that have been blocked from me, stolen, or delayed. I pray for total physical and spiritual restoration, and I forbid the enemy from ever assaulting my body again. I bind and send to the abyss all demons that physically attack me. I bind and send to the abyss all demonic forces enforcing this now-broken covenant. In Jesus' name, I pray. Amen.*

The unholy covenant she made was broken, and the physical attacks on her stopped. GLORY TO GOD!!

VERY IMPORTANT: After breaking an unholy covenant, please be mindful of your dreams. The enemy often tries to reestablish unholy covenants through dreams. If that happens, pray the *"Prayer to Break Unholy Covenants"* for several days.

The enemy's tactics are cunning, so as a precaution, I usually pray the *"Prayer to Break Unholy Covenants"* three or more times a month, just to be sure I haven't unwittingly reestablished a demonic covenant through a forgotten dream or through some other point of entry. I try to block as many access points to the enemy as possible.

Note: The enemy needs legal grounds (i.e., a covenant, an agreement) to attack a Christian physically. He won't just walk up and ask for it, but he will obtain it through points of entry, like dreams (See the "Dreams" section in this book), thoughts, demonic games, and occult activities such as Ouija boards, séances; tarot cards, psychic readings, or palm readings; witchcraft, sorcery, crystals, charms, statues, and relics of false gods, etc.

The end goal of the enemy is to steal, kill, and destroy (John 10:10). He is completely merciless and devoid of love. Show no mercy to the enemy. Get him out of your life.

Prayer to Break Unholy Covenants

~~~

Dear Lord,

I put my trust in You. Let me never be put to shame. Deliver me in Your righteousness and cause me to escape. Incline Your ear to me and save me. (Psalm 71:1-2)

Lord, I acknowledge my sins and ask You for forgiveness.

I pray for wisdom to avoid unholy covenants, curses, traps, and snares, but if I fall, I trust in You to lift me up and lead me to safety, for You are my refuge and strength, a very present help in trouble.

In the name and by the power of Jesus Christ, I renounce and break all unholy covenants and agreements that I have made knowingly or unknowingly, awake or in my dreams. I repent for making those covenants, and I close all open doors used by satanic forces to access and affect my life. *(Repeat 2x)*

I plead the blood of Jesus upon myself and proclaim that I am free from all forms of evil oppression. I bind and send to the abyss all familiar spirits and demonic forces that execute unholy covenants, curses, hexes, spells, potions, charms, demonic altars, evil desires, spiritual thefts, ritual sacrifices, or other wicked enchantments and devices against me.

Dear Lord, please restore me fully and completely. Bless me to recover all that I have lost spiritually and physically. Give me beauty for ashes and joy for sorrow.

Lead me not into temptation but deliver me from evil. Enlighten me and grant me peace in my life that passes all understanding.

Thank You, Father. In Jesus' name, I pray. Amen.

Psalm 71:1-2 & 46:1, James 1:5, Isaiah 61:3, Matthew 6:13, Psalm 18:28, Philippians 4:7

Prayer to Break/Cut Soul Ties

~~~

The prayer below is to break soul ties with someone with whom you have been intimate outside of a marriage covenant.

Father in heaven,

You are holy and righteous, merciful, and forgiving. If You, Lord, should mark iniquities, who could stand? But there is forgiveness with You that You may be feared. (Psalm 130:3-4)

Lord, I repent for my sins and ask for Your forgiveness. Please cleanse me and restore my soul.

By the power of Jesus Christ, I declare that all unholy ties, covenants, and connections to my soul are broken.

I break all unholy covenants I have entered into through fornication, adultery, or by any other means. I cut all soul ties between me and *(name(s))*. I choose to forgive any partners who hurt or offended me.

I bind and send to the abyss all demons and evil forces affecting me and connected to me because of sexual relations outside of marriage. I command the enemy to release me and get out of my life right now, in the mighty name of Jesus!

I reclaim all my virtues and every gift, blessing, and reward that has been stolen from me by spiritual thieves. I command their return now!

I pray for all my soul fractures to be healed, repaired, and restored.

Father, I thank You for Your mercy and forgiveness, and I thank You for breaking all my soul ties. In Jesus' name, I pray. Amen.

Psalm 130:3-4, Psalm 23:3

Important: In order to heal and free yourself from the other person(s) and completely let go, you <u>must</u> forgive them and release them using your words.

Curses

~~~

Curses cannot hurt you unless you deserve them.
They are like birds that fly by and never light.
Proverbs 26:2 GNT

Curse: Oppose, fight, destroy; crush.

What is a curse?

A curse is an unfavorable decree spoken against a person, place, or thing. It often leads to receiving less than the best God has to offer. If a person, place, or thing is cursed, they *(or it)* will experience recurring opposition, destruction, misfortune, adversity, undesirable outcomes, frequent disappointments, crushing blows, unexplainable upsets, tragic occurrences, losses, sicknesses, diseases, stagnation, lack, or death until the curse is lifted.

Curses come from one of two sources: God or humans. They don't pop up out of nowhere, and they don't land unless they are deserved *(Proverbs 26:2).* No one wants to be under a curse, and the best way to avoid them is to obey God. So, let's focus on lifting and removing curses.

Curses from God.

Curses from God are self-inflicted, self-earned judgments or consequences for sinful actions. In most cases, the cursed person was given ample opportunities to repent and self-correct, but they did not.

A few examples of actions and choices that may result in a curse from God are below:

- Idol worship, murder, theft, adultery; bearing false witness, dishonoring parents, taking the Lord's name in vain *(Exodus 20:3-17)*

43

- Taking holy communion unworthily *(1 Corinthians 11:29)*
- Touching God's anointed and doing His prophets harm *(See Psalm 105:15 and 1 Chronicles 16:22)*
- Engaging in witchcraft, sorcery, divination, or other occult practices *(Deuteronomy 18:10-11, Galatians 5:19-20)*

A curse from God can affect an individual or an entire family. One example unfolds in 2 Samuel 12:1-19, where David—both a man of God and the King of Israel—conspired to orchestrate the death of Uriah the Hittite *(a highly respected soldier)* during battle. After Uriah's death, David married Bathsheba, Uriah's widow, who was already pregnant with David's child. The whole thing started when David coveted another man's wife *(Bathsheba)*. That sin led to adultery, and that sin led to murder, and that sin led to a curse from God who sees all.

Nothing in all creation is hidden from God's sight. Everything is uncovered and laid bare before the eyes of Him to whom we must give account. (Hebrews 4:13)

David had to give an account for his actions.

Curses upon David from the Lord

Thus says the Lord: Behold, I will raise up adversity against you from your own house; and I will take your wives before your eyes and give them to your neighbor, and he shall lie with your wives in the sight of this sun. For you did it secretly, but I will do this thing before all Israel, before the sun. The child also who is born to you shall surely die. (2 Samuel 12:11-14)

Just as the Lord said, there was much adversity in David's house. Amnon *(David's son)* raped his half-sister Tamar, and then her brother Absalom *(also David's son)* killed Amnon … and WOW! This is a must-read true story if you're interested *(2 Samuel 13:1-32)*.

The Bible is full of great, truthful accounts that are relevant today and provide insight into God's ways, His love, His mercy, and also His judgments for disobedience.

Just as the Lord said, King David's wives *(concubines)* were lain with by his neighbor *(his own son)* right out under the open sun before all of Israel *(2 Samuel 16:21-22).* Not to mention that David and Bathsheba's first child died according to the word of the Lord spoken by His prophet Nathan. *(2 Samuel 12:18)*

Generational curse upon David's family

> *[Thus says the Lord] You have killed Uriah the Hittite with the sword; you have taken his wife to be your wife ... Now, therefore, the sword shall never depart from your house ...* (2 Samuel 12:9-10)
>
> *See "Generational Curses" to learn more.*

What can be done to lift a curse from God?

> *"Even from eternity, I am He, and there is no one who can rescue from My hand; I act, and who can revoke or reverse it?" Says the Lord.* (Isaiah 43:13 AMP)

No one has the power to overturn God's judgments. When faced with a curse or other consequences from God, the only appropriate response is to **repent** and ask for mercy.

God's mercy and grace are needed to lift His curse and be restored. Thus says the Lord:

> *I will return again to My place until they **acknowledge their guilt and seek My face** ...* (Hosea 5:15 ESV)

The above Scripture implies that the Lord is waiting for something. He is waiting for an admission of guilt. **REPENT** and seek His face in prayer.

To repent means to express sincere remorse to God for sinful thoughts, intentions, and behaviors. Repentance also requires a change of heart, mind, and actions.

After you have repented, humbly and reverently ask the Lord for mercy. Ask Him to remove any curses on you *(your family, business, ministry, etc.)*. Ask the Lord to help you change. Then submit to the Holy Spirit. He will lead and guide you. He will help you renew your mind so that your desires and actions align with God's commandments. Turn away from the *"flash, bang, pow"* and foolishness of this world. Do not desire to do as the world does, and please do not idolize celebrities, sports figures, or other humans. Accept God's ways to avoid sin and avoid a curse. Commit to righteousness. It's part of your spiritual armor—the breastplate of righteousness *(Ephesians 6:14)*. Follow Jesus!

Curses Decreed by Humans.

This is a curse spoken by one human being upon another, often because of an offense, but sometimes, just out of evil, jealousy, hate, or spite. Since the Lord did not authorize the curse, you can easily break it. This is a devilish curse that seeks to exercise control over your life or destiny. It is a curse that an individual *(often a witch or other occult worker)* pronounces on a person, place or thing.

The curse may be spoken against a person, place, or thing, but the person speaking the curse *(the curser)* cannot enforce it. The curser must be connected to familiar spirits and demons who mobilize to carry out evil. The curser may connect with evil spirits by performing ritual sacrifices, setting up demonic altars, burning voodoo candles, repeating incantations, or by any number of unholy practices to solidify their covenant with the forces of evil.

Have no fear, Jesus is here!

Jesus is our hero! He defeated all the forces of evil, including Satan. Jesus defeated the demonic powers that carry out unauthorized curses, and so can we. As followers of Christ, Jesus gave us power over all the power of the enemy *(Luke 10:19).* Those who speak ungodly curses upon us and the demons they summon are our enemies. The Lord does not permit us to take revenge on people, but we can defeat the demons they send to harm us.

How to lift a curse placed on you by a human (not God).

1. **Cancel the curse.** Use your own words to say it is canceled.
2. **Bind and send away the demons and familiar spirits invoked to carry out the curse.**
3. **Believe it's done,** thanks to our Lord Jesus.

Pray the following "Prayer to Break Curses" in this book.

Prayer to Break Curses

~~~

(Pray this to break curses over your life spoken by other humans. Use the "Mercy Prayer to Lift a Curse" to pray for the removal of God's curses.)

Father in heaven,

Deliver me from the hand of the wicked, from the grasp of those who are evil and cruel. For You have been my hope, Sovereign Lord, and my confidence. (Psalm 71:4-5 NIV)

Lord, I repent for my sins and ask for Your forgiveness. I thank You for the blood of Jesus that covers and protects me.

By the power of Jesus Christ, I take authority and cast down, cancel, and revoke any curses, negative words, witchcraft, incantations, hexes, evil enchantments, and spells spoken and directed at me.

I bind and send to the abyss all demons and familiar spirits summoned to enforce curses, spells, demonic altars, ritual sacrifices, or other evil enchantments and commands against me. *(Repeat 2x)*

- I cancel all curses spoken over my family's bloodline by witches, sorcerers, or other human beings.
- I cancel all curses I may have received from touching unholy objects, accepting or picking up strange money, or eating foods that were cursed.

Dear Lord, I ask You to overthrow all rulers, powers, and authorities in the heavens that support any curses directed at me *(and my family)*.

I repent for, renounce, and break all unholy covenants and agreements that I may have entered into knowingly or unknowingly, while awake or asleep. I also close all doors and portals used by the enemy to afflict or harm me in any way and in any area of my life.

Let every occult device being used to watch, monitor, or target me become faulty, broken, and destroyed.

(Restoration)

I now reclaim any blessings that have been blocked from me, stolen, or delayed. I pray for total physical and spiritual restoration, and I forbid the enemy from retaliating against me.

Dear Lord, please bless me so that I recover anything I may have lost. Bless me with rewards, breakthroughs, opportunities, wealth, excellent health, and spiritual growth.

Let me experience Your best. Give me beauty for ashes and joy for sorrow. Restore me fully and completely, and grant me peace that passes all understanding.

In Jesus' name, I pray. Amen.

Psalm 71:4-5, Isaiah 61:3, Philippians 4:7

Note: Unholy covenants are contracts with the enemy that give him legal permission to access and affect our lives.

Mercy Prayer to Lift a Curse

~~~

This prayer is to lift a God-ordained curse off your life.
Please read "Curses" for more understanding.

Dear Lord,

It is written in Your word that *"He who covers his sins will not prosper, but whoever confesses and forsakes them will have mercy."* Proverbs 28:13 NKJV

Lord, I need Your mercy. I will not hide my sins, but I will confess them and forsake them. Please forgive me for the following sins:

(Be truthful with God and confess your sins here. Some examples are listed below to get you started. Confess all that apply, and add others, as needed.)

Adultery, fornication, rape, murder, human trafficking, gambling, witchcraft, sorcery, divination, theft, idol worship, abortion, incest, homosexuality, bestiality, touching God's anointed or His prophets, taking Holy communion unworthily, cursing Israel, dishonoring parents.

Father, I have confessed my sins. Please have mercy on me. I relinquish pride and request Your help to change. I submit to the Holy Spirit to renew my mind and transform me. Create in me a clean heart so that I may please You.

Please remove all curses from my life. Restore me and bless me. Give me a heart to do Your will and increase my desire to bring glory to Your name. I believe in Your mercy, Lord, and I thank You for extending it to me. I believe the curses are lifted off of my life. Bless You, Father.

In Jesus' name, I pray. Amen.

Proverbs 28:13, Genesis 12:3, Numbers 24:1-9, Romans 12:2, Psalm 51:10

Generational Curses

~~~

Generational curses *(i.e., consequences)* are real, and they are passed down from generation to generation within a family. These consequences ripple across families, duplicating negative patterns and producing the same undesirable results for decades. Sadly, the struggles some people face result from evil forces following their bloodlines, like spiritual bloodhounds sent to enforce unholy pacts and covenants forged in times past. The Bible records a generational curse that was placed on the family of Eli the priest:

Now the sons of Eli [the priest] were corrupt, they did not know the Lord (1 Samuel 2:12).

Now Eli was very old, and he heard everything his sons did to all Israel, and how they lay with the women who assembled at the door of the tabernacle of meeting.

*So, Eli said to them, "Why do you do such things?... No, my sons! For it is not a good report that I hear. **You make the Lord's people transgress."** (1 Samuel 2:22-24)*

Yet, they did not listen to their father, so the Lord decreed:

The time is coming when I will kill all the young men in your family and your clan so that no man in your family will live to be old. You will be troubled and look with envy on all the blessings I will give to the other people of Israel, but no one in your family will ever again live to old age.

*Yet I will keep one of your descendants alive... But he will become blind and lose all hope, and all your other descendants will die a violent death. **When your two sons Hophni and Phinehas both*** *die on the same day, this will show you that everything I have said will come true.* (1 Samuel 2:31-34 GNT)

So, did it come true? Yes, it did. According to the decreed word of the Lord, Hophni, and Phinehas, the two sons of Eli, the priest, died on the same day *(1 Samuel 4:11).* Their immoral conduct rained down a generational curse that would follow the men in their family for generations.

How to Break a Generational Curse from God

True story. Years ago, when I began trying to break generational curses off my life, I found and repeated prayers used by ministers I held in high esteem. I called out the sins of my ancestors that I was aware of, and I renounced and repented of them. Then, as instructed, **I declared** that all generational curses were broken off my life and my children's lives.

What was the result? Well, I got relief from demonic oppression by denouncing certain spirits, but the generational curse—the overarching one—just didn't seem to be broken.

Fast forward a few years. When I began writing this book, the Lord instructed me to include a prayer to break generational curses. He inspired Lamentations 3:22-23 as the Scripture to begin the prayer. I was perplexed since that is a mercy Scripture. It didn't fit the direction that I had seen and used in the past when praying for the removal of generational curses. I was taught that I could declare the removal and cancellation of generational curses. So, I didn't understand why the Holy Spirit started the prayer with a mercy Scripture, but I kept it because I trust Him, and I knew that through this, He was going to teach me something. I drafted the prayer, and I read it before the Lord, waiting for His approval—waiting for His anointing; but lo and behold, **there was no anointing!** *Oh no!* This was a big problem because the anointing breaks the yoke *(the burden, the oppression, the bondage),* and the whole purpose of this prayer, and all prayers in this book is to break yokes. *(Isaiah 10:27)*

Stop the presses!! I could not move forward without God's approval and anointing.

I stopped writing for a few days, during which time I fasted, prayed, and asked the Lord what was wrong. What had I missed? I needed His direction, correction, and guidance. I needed His anointing to continue. If not, my plan was to shut it all down; but days later, He responded.

The Lord asked me, *"If I decree a curse, who can break it?"*

I humbly answered, *"No one, Lord."*

Ahh! **That was my answer!** The Holy Spirit was correct when He started the prayer with a "mercy" Scripture *(Lamentations 3:22-23).* The generational curse prayer needed to be a prayer to request mercy instead of a prayer declaring and decreeing that God's curses were removed. **No one can lift a curse that God decrees.** No human being has the power to override His judgments. The best we can do is pray for His mercy. So, I deleted the declarations of curse removal and presented it to the Lord again. Alas, the anointing! *Praise the Lord!* I resumed writing.

See the *"Prayer to Break Generational Curses."*

How to Break Generational Curses Cast by Witches

If a witch or sorcerer places a curse on your family, you have the power to break it *(See Prayer to Break Curses).* Thanks to Jesus, your power is greater than that of witches *(1 John 4:4, Luke 10:19).* You have the power to override man's curses, but not God's.

Prayer to Break Generational Curses

Fast and pray to request generational curses be lifted.

~~~

Dear heavenly Father,

It is because of Your mercies that we are not consumed because Your compassions fail not. They are new every morning. Great is Your faithfulness. (Lamentations 3:22-23)

Lord, I believe my life has been affected by the sins of my ancestors and also by the consequences of my own sins.

I confess and repent for my sins and for the sins of my ancestors.

I repent for our unfaithfulness and hostility toward You throughout the years, for You have been faithful. You are holy, righteous, and merciful. You are mighty God, and Your mercy endures forever.

I renounce and break all unholy covenants that my ancestors and I have made knowingly or unknowingly over the last four generations.

I acknowledge our guilt, Lord, and I seek Your face for mercy to lift any and all generational curses from my family's bloodlines.

I choose to forgive and release everyone who has hurt, wronged or offended me in any way.

Lord, please forgive the iniquity of Your people. Please take away all Your wrath and turn from the fierceness of Your anger. Forgive us, O God of our salvation, and cause Your anger toward us to cease.

Will You be angry with us forever? Will You draw out Your anger to all generations? Will You not revive us again that Your people may rejoice in You? Show us Your mercy, O Lord, and grant us Your salvation.

Be merciful, O Lord, and give ear to my request. For You are good and ready to forgive and plenteous in mercy to all who call upon You.

I trust that You have heard my prayer, Lord, and that all generational curses will be broken off my family's bloodlines according to Your mercy and will.

I bless You and thank You for lifting and removing generational curses and for healing and restoring my family and me fully and completely in all areas of our lives.

Help us to do Your will, Lord. Bless us, and cause us to prosper, and experience Your best, Lord.

In Jesus' name, I pray. Amen.

Lamentations 3:22-23, Leviticus 26:40 and 44 (NIV), Hosea 5:15, Psalm 85:2-7, Psalm 86:3-5

About Troubling Dreams

~~~

A young lady contacted me following a series of troubling dreams that she experienced over the course of three nights. In one dream, she was running from someone who was throwing knives at her. The next night, she had a similar dream in which someone was shooting at her with a gun. On the third night, she was being chased by someone swinging a machete! To make matters worse, she woke up with a serious headache after each dream.

In all three dreams, the young lady managed to escape unharmed, but the dreams left her unsettled, and also suffering from a headache. I sought the Lord, and He instructed me to do the following:

Step One—Provide knowledge.

My people are destroyed for lack of knowledge... (Hosea 4:6)

If you have a dream wherein you are threatened or wounded with a gun, cannon, darts, bow-and-arrow, knife, sling blade, machete, ax, sword, or another weapon—this is a blaring alarm that there is a bull's eye on your back by someone in the occult. They have marked you as a target, and they are directing evil forces *(weapons)* at you. Please do not be frightened. The Lord Jesus can protect you!

You'll want to engage in spiritual warfare after having this type of dream, even if you can't imagine anyone has bad intentions toward you. *(Pray the "Prayer After a Dream with Weapons.")*

So, I shared with the mannerable young lady that her dreams indicated that someone involved in the occult had summoned and directed demonic forces toward her. She may not have done anything at all to them. You don't have to. The enemy hates all mankind, even those who follow him and do his evil bidding.

Step Two—Engage in Successful Spiritual Warfare.

What constitutes successful spiritual warfare?... **RESULTS**.

I led us both in prayer to repent for our sins, and then I cast down all demonic words spoken against the young lady. I bound and sent to the abyss all demons and familiar spirits that had been summoned to enforce evil curses, spells, hexes, ritual sacrifices, demonic altars, witchcraft, sorcery, and other occult activities against her.

I also asked her to forgive others—whoever came to mind. I instructed her to start by saying, *"I choose to forgive (name)."*

Next, I taught her how to break any unholy covenants that she may have entered into, and together, we broke them. *(See "Prayer to Break Unholy Covenants.")*

Finally, I prayed for her to be fully restored.

Step Three—Deal with That Headache.

Following our prayer, I bound up the headache spirit and cast it off of the young lady. ***Wait! What?***... Did I just bind up a headache spirit? Yes, I did. At this point, you might be saying, *"You are going too far! Everything is not a demon."* I understand that thought. Really, I do. If it were not for the experience I'm about to share, I would agree with you wholeheartedly. Let me explain.

Years ago, while serving on the ministerial staff of a church in Atlanta, Georgia (USA), an upset grandmother approached me in the restroom. Church service was over, and I was drying my hands at the sink when she approached me with her little grandson at her side. The little one was about five years old. He had a sad look on his precious little face, and his little eyes were droopy, nearly closed. I could tell he didn't feel well. The grandmother asked me to pray for him. She said that he had been suffering from a headache for days and medicine was not helping. The other kids were outside the church running and playing, but he was in too much pain to join them.

So, I looked at the child, preparing to lay hands on him and pray, when all of a sudden, the Lord opened my eyes in the spirit, and I could see, right there standing with one foot on each of the child's shoulders, was a little demon—about two feet tall—pounding on the child's head like a drum! *Bang! Bang! Bang!* That demon was pounding, one fist after another on both sides of the child's head. I shook off my astonishment and focused on ministering to the little child, saying something like:

"I bind you, demon, and command you to get off of this child right now, in the name of Jesus!" Then I saw the demon instantly jump off of his shoulders and disappear.

The grandmother looked at me with disappointment and said, *"I don't want that! I want you to pray for him."* While I was explaining to her what had just happened, the boy slipped out of the restroom unnoticed. Panicked, we both rushed out of the restroom to look for him, and there he was—outside—playing with the other kids. In fact, he was laughing and climbing a tree! His little face was no longer sad; it was glowing, and his droopy eyes now sparkled. He was healed! Thank You, Jesus!

His grandmother went over to the tree and called him to come down. He obeyed and she asked him if his head still hurt. He said "no," and then ran off to continue playing with the other kids. His head was no longer hurting. The headache was gone, and he was happy. As for Grandma… well, she, too, put on a big smile and was thankful. God received the glory!

So, the Lord enlightened me that day, and I learned that some headaches—**NOT ALL**—may be caused by a little demon pounding on the head.

(Note: If you have a headache, please do not hesitate to seek medical attention if needed.)

Conclusion

I followed up with the young lady, and after a year, she reported that she had no more targeted dreams, no calamities, and no more headaches after we prayed! Praise the Lord!

Greater is He (Jesus) that is in you than he (the enemy) that is in the world. 1 John 4:4 (KJV)

Just like the young lady, I've had dreams with weapons targeting me, and I haven't always escaped unharmed. I have been struck by a bullet, bitten by a dog, and in one dream, I was shot in the leg with a bow-and-arrow. Thankfully, in other dreams with weapons, I managed to escape unharmed.

Whether you are injured in the dream or not, protect yourself. Jesus gave you power and authority, so use your authority! *(Luke 10:19)* The warfare prayers in this book are to assist you in defeating the enemy safely. Fight for your best life in Christ!

Prayer After a Troubling Dream

~~~

Sometimes, we have dreams that we can't remember, yet we are troubled when we wake up. This prayer seeks to address any issues that could arise after troubling dreams. It's a prayer of multiple protections.

Our Father, which art in heaven,

Hallowed be Your name. *The whole earth is filled with awe at Your wonders.* You are holy and righteous. *You make the dawn and the sunset shout for joy! (Psalm 65:8 NIV & AMP)*

Lord, I confess that I have sinned in thoughts, deeds, and intentions, and I repent. Please forgive me and help me to forgive others.

In the name of Jesus Christ, I bind and send to the abyss all demons and familiar spirits that were present in any of my dreams.

Dear Lord, I ask You to overthrow all rulers, powers, and authorities in the heavens that are blocking or delaying my progress, success, blessings, rewards, breakthroughs, spiritual growth, promotions, healing, or anything else.

I bind and cancel any harmful and ungodly effects, outcomes, or results from snakes, animals, insects, foods, beings, entities, objects, or persons—dead or alive—that appeared in any of my dreams.

I renounce and break all unholy covenants and agreements that I may have entered into knowingly or unknowingly, while awake or asleep.

I confound and cancel any planned attacks by the enemy or by any persons toward me, *my family,* my job, my residence, *business, ministry,* vehicle(s), *property, investments,* and possessions.

I bind any demons around my vehicle(s) and send them to the abyss. I pray the Lord will protect me from accidents, injuries, thefts, car jackings, and threats of any kind.

I destroy all arrows, bullets, cannons, knives, hatchets, or other weapons shot, swung, thrown, or aimed at me in any of my dreams.

I proclaim that no weapons formed against me shall prosper. I shall not die but I shall live an abundant life and declare the works of the Lord.

- I expel *(spiritually)* all foods presented or consumed in my dreams and I bind and send to the abyss all evil spirits attached to those foods. No harm shall come to me from unholy foods presented or consumed in any of my dreams.
- I proclaim that I shall experience no losses, no sicknesses, no diseases, no afflictions, no setbacks, or death because of unholy foods presented or consumed in any of my dreams.
- I bind and send to the abyss all demons sent to steal, kill, and destroy me, *my family, my marriage,* my relationships, my health, home, safety, security, income, destiny, spiritual growth, peace, freedom, and all other areas of my life.
- I bind and send to the abyss all unholy agents sent to enforce curses, hexes, evil words, ritual sacrifices, demonic altars, spells, charms, potions, incantations, or other evil enchantments and occult activities directed at me.

Save me from my enemies, Lord, and guard me from the evil one. In Jesus' name, I pray. Amen.

Psalm 65:8 (NIV & AMP), Isaiah 54:17, Psalm 118:17, Luke 10:19, Psalm 59:1, 2 Thessalonians 3:3

Prayer After a Dream with Weapons

~~~

Please pay attention to dreams in which you are being pursued with a weapon such as a gun, knife, or other. Trouble may follow on the job or in business, ministry, health, family, marriage, school, or other areas after this type of dream. Pray this prayer repeatedly, three or more times a week, for at least two weeks following a dream with weapons. Be sure to repent and always ask the Lord to help you forgive others.

Dear Lord,

You are my refuge and strength—a very present help in the time of trouble. (Psalm 46:1)

I acknowledge my sins and ask You to forgive me. I plead the blood of Jesus and put up a hedge of protection around myself.

I bind and send to the abyss all demons, and familiar spirits that were present in my dream(s).

I revoke all forms of witchcraft, sorcery, and divination aimed at me.

- I destroy every demonic entity, bullet, arrow, cannon, knife, hatchet, machete, ax, gun, or other weapon that was aimed, shot, hurled, pointed, swung, or otherwise directed at me in my dream(s).
- I bind and send to the abyss every unholy entity summoned against me to carry out curses, unholy covenants, spells, hexes, incantations, potions, charms, witchcraft, sorcery, demonic altars, ritual sacrifices, evil enchantments, or other evil commands.

- I deactivate all demonic altars, magic mirrors, and other occult instruments used to summon and direct unholy forces toward me. Let those altars and devices fail that are used for evil.
- I bind and send to the abyss all evil forces called upon to negatively affect my life, *my children, marriage,* my spiritual growth, my health, my income, my mental faculties, or my progress in any way.

I choose to forgive my enemies for vengeance is the Lord's. He will repay.

I proclaim that no weapons formed against me shall prosper and I shall live a blessed and abundant life.

Be merciful to me, Lord, and restore me completely. Hide me under the shadow of Your wings. I call upon You Lord, for You are worthy to be praised. So, shall I be saved from my enemies.

In Jesus' name, I pray. Amen.

Psalm 46:1, Matthew 5:44, Romans 12:19, Isaiah 54:17, Psalm 57:1, Psalm 17:8, Psalm 18:3

Understanding Dreams with Food or Eating

~~~

When food is presented in a dream, there is a strong likelihood that the enemy is near. It may seem like an innocent dream, but beware. The enemy has been deceiving humans since the days of Adam and Eve. He is a master of deception. He cleverly uses dreams, objects, cards, cuss words, covenants, false religions, secret societies, crystals, trinkets, money, ambition, and more to introduce evil forces into our lives.

If you see or eat food in a dream, please take immediate preventive measures to block unpleasant results. When food is present in a dream, the enemy is trying to do one or all of the following:

1. Plant unholy spiritual foods into your body to cause health issues, which may include chronic illnesses, cancer, respiratory or bronchial illness, memory issues, diseases, or loss of energy among a number of other ailments.

2. Form an unholy covenant with you to gain legal entry into your life and affairs to cause disappointments, unfulfilled dreams, loss of job, loss of income, loss of important deals or closings, blocked promotions, blocked raises, or other opportunity losses.

3. Cause inner turmoil such as discouragement or depression, loss of interest in the Bible or the things of God. You may also lose interest in your spouse or family unit; loss of joy, hope, or motivation; anger toward God, or other forms of internal conflict.

Satan wants to steal, kill, and destroy you and any progress you are making, but do not fear! Use your spiritual warfare prayers.

Greater is He [the Lord] who is in you, than he [the devil] that is in the world. (1 John 4:4)

Food dreams may be the result of a direct attack from Satan or the result of someone practicing witchcraft or sorcery against you. Either way, you want to expel the spiritual food immediately to stop the intended evil effects of food in your dreams.

Remember to pray several times a week for at least two weeks after a dream with food.

Prayer After a Dream with Food

~~~

Pray this immediately after having a food dream.

Father in heaven,

I will praise You with my whole heart and tell of all Your marvelous works. I will be glad and rejoice in You and sing praises to Your name for You are The Most High. (From Psalm 9:1-2)

Lord, I confess my sins and ask for Your forgiveness.

In the name of Jesus Christ, I bind and send to the abyss all demonic entities and familiar spirits that were present in any of my dreams.

I renounce, break, and destroy all unholy covenants, contracts, and agreements that I have made while awake or asleep.

I revoke all forms of witchcraft, sorcery, and divination aimed at me.

I plead the blood of Jesus and pray for a hedge of protection around myself in the mighty name of Jesus!

(Spiritually purge unholy foods)

- **I expel *(spiritually)* all foods consumed in my dreams, and I bind and send to the abyss all evil spirits attached to those foods. *(Repeat 2x)***

- I bind and send to the abyss all evil forces sent to block my blessings, bring troubles into my life, upset my destiny, or cause me to be sick and diseased.

- I ask the Lord to overthrow all rulers, powers, and authorities in the heavens that are warring against, blocking, delaying, or hindering my progress, blessings, and breakthroughs in any way.

- I bind and send to the abyss all demons and familiar spirits that have been summoned to carry out evil words, evil wishes, evil desires, evil plots, demonic altars, occult sacrifices, spells, charms, hexes, potions, incantations, witchcraft, sorcery, and divination toward my health, wealth, progress, job, *children, spouse, marriage, relationships, destiny, appearance,* or any other areas of my life.

I proclaim that:

- No weapons formed against me shall prosper, and nothing shall by any means hurt me.
- I shall suffer no losses, no sicknesses, no diseases, no afflictions, no setbacks, or death because of unholy foods presented or eaten in my dreams.
- I will not experience harmful effects—physically or spiritually—from eating unholy foods in my dreams.
- I will not lose anything, including favor, jobs, offers, promotions, raises, contracts, deals, closings, sales, or other opportunities.
- I shall not die but live life abundantly and declare the works of the Lord.

Lord, please make all grace abound toward me so that I, having all sufficiency in all things, may abound and have more than enough for every good work, according to Your word.

In Jesus' name, I pray. Amen.

Psalm 9:1-2, Isaiah 54:17, Luke 10:19, Psalm 118:17 (NKJV), 2 Corinthians 9:8

Understanding Snake Dreams

~~~

Behold, I give unto you power to tread on serpents (snakes) and scorpions, and over all the power of the enemy: and nothing shall by any means hurt you. (Luke 10:19)

The night before a loved one was scheduled to undergo surgery, I had a troubling dream. In the dream, my loved one was in the front seat, on the passenger side, of a small car. The car had an open sunroof. The day was sunny and bright. I could see my loved one in the passenger seat facing forward, brave and ready to go to the hospital for surgery, but I couldn't see who was in the driver's seat.

In an instant, a king-sized yellow snake brought its head up straight through the open sunroof. This snake was massive! Its head was so big and thick that it could barely fit through the open sunroof! Then the snake—with its head high above the sunroof—turned from left to right, looking around for something. Then, it lowered its massive head back into the seat next to my loved one. That's when I realized the snake was the driver! It was planning to go with my loved one to the hospital!

I immediately woke up from the dream. I had to pray. My loved one was having surgery later that day, and that dream revealed that he was going into surgery with a dangerous constrictor at his side.

In most cases, spiritual snakes do not show up without someone having sent them. So, I bound up the snake, cut off its head, and threw its carcass *(spiritually)* into the abyss using my words.

Now that the snake was destroyed, it could no longer present danger to my loved one. I prayed that the Lord would send angels into that operating room with my loved one. I also prayed for the Lord to lead and guide the medical professionals so there would be no mishaps during surgery. I fasted and prayed for a successful surgery. Praise the

Lord! The surgery was successful and devoid of complications, and the healing and recovery were much quicker than expected.

As for the person who sent the snake... I have no idea who it was, and I dared not to speculate, but God knew, and I turned them over to God. Vengeance is the Lord's. He will repay. Those who practice evil will reap what they have sown, according to God's word. The Lord watches over His word to perform it, so you may rest assured they got theirs. Though they practice evil, God still loves them. As a Father, He alone is able to correct them and, in many cases, change them. I know a few former witches who turned their lives over to Christ. As representatives of Christ, we are to forgive and walk in love.

Personally, I have had countless dreams with snakes in them, and the snakes usually targeted me instead of my loved ones. When I was a babe in Christ, I had a snake coiled up in my stomach. I didn't know what was wrong with me. I would get sick and nauseous and find it hard to stand. I would be fine for one minute, and the next, I could barely stand for weakness. I went to visit my doctor. He said I was a normal, healthy twenty-something. He could find nothing wrong. I inquired of the Lord, and He sent me to my pastor's wife *(she was also a pastor)*. With one look, she saw a *(spiritual)* snake coiled up in my stomach, and she commanded it to come out of my body. I could feel it uncoiling, and then it was gone. My weeks-long saga had ended, and I was no longer afflicted in that way. Through the years, I have helped many others experiencing the same issue. We truly have power over serpents and scorpions and over all the power of the enemy. Thank You, Jesus!

If a snake is present in your dream, pull out your prayers. Snakes are often representatives of Satan, and they warn of deception, treachery, or possible troubles. Pray the *"Prayer After a Dream with Snakes."*

Fight for your best life in Christ!

Prayer After a Dream with Snakes

~~~

Father God,

I bless You. No one is holy like You, Lord, for there is none besides You, nor is there any rock like our God. (1 Samuel 2:2)

Lord, I repent for my sins and ask You to forgive me.

I exercise my authority to trample on serpents and scorpions and over all the power of the enemy, and nothing shall by any means hurt me.

- I bind and send to the abyss every snake, viper, python[1], cottonmouth[2], cobra, or other serpent appearing in my dreams, including those that constrict my progress and success, or block my breakthroughs, inhibit my growth, interfere with my health, wealth, and well-being, or cause me to suffer loss or go backward.

- I renounce, break, and destroy all unholy covenants, contracts, and agreements that I have entered into knowingly or unknowingly, awake or in my dreams, and I close all open doors used by the enemy to afflict me in any way.

- I cancel, cast down, and revoke any witchcraft, sorcery, divination, spells, hexes, charms, voodoo, incantations, and evil enchantments spoken against me.

- I bind and send to the abyss all demonic forces and familiar spirits sent to carry out curses, covenants, spells, hexes, witchcraft, sorcery, divination, or other occult commands and activities against me.

By the power of Jesus Christ, I command all serpents around me, attached to me, inside of me[3], or in any way affecting me, to depart from me, release me, go away from me, and never return! *(Repeat 2x)*

I bind and send to the abyss all unholy spirits on assignment to cause me sickness, disease, death, accidents, hardships, financial troubles, relationship, *marriage,* or family troubles, lack of favor, stagnation, tragedy, losses, and any other afflictions.

Let my enemies be confounded, repented, defeated, and retreated.

I plead the blood of Jesus upon myself and proclaim that no weapons formed against me shall prosper.

Lord Jesus, please bless me. Restore everything the enemy has taken to delay my progress, success, and breakthroughs. Restore everything that has been blocked, withheld, or stolen from me.

In Jesus' name, I pray. Amen.

1 Samuel 2:2, Luke 10:19, Ephesians 6:12, Isaiah 54:17

[1] The python snake is a constrictor that squeezes or suffocates its victims. Python is often associated with money and health issues, though it may negatively affect other areas because it is evil.

[2] The cottonmouth snake is an opportunist and can cause unexpected accidents, unexplainable falls, and injuries, which may seem like freak accidents. Though it may attack anyone, the cottonmouth may be attached to persons considered "accident-prone."

[3] A snake sent through witchcraft or sorcery may coil up in the stomach of a targeted individual. It can cause stomach nausea, discomfort, and sickness that doctors cannot diagnose with certainty.

Dreams About the Deceased

~~~

Beware, saints! The enemy can exploit your vulnerability while you sleep by appearing as one of your deceased loved ones, a friend, or an acquaintance. A dream in which a deceased person appears is a very strong indicator that a demon is trying to enter your life.

The being in your dream was not your relative, friend, or acquaintance. It was a demon pretending to be the deceased person to make you lower your guard and welcome it. Most often, the spirit will not speak in the dream, but as soon as you welcome it—it gains legal entry to your life, destiny, health, money, family, and circumstances without any resistance. However, you can kick it out! *(See the "Prayer After Dreams About the Deceased.")*

What's Really Going on with This Dream?

While our relatives or others have passed on, the demons who lurked around in their lives did not die. Those demonic spirits are still out to steal, kill, and destroy, and they need warm *(alive)* bodies. We, who are alive, are the new targets for destruction, but we don't have to be. We can stop them.

A relative of mine passed away, and weeks later, a living relative had a dream where the deceased person appeared but did not speak. That unholy visitation was an alert that a demon, familiar with and connected to the family, was looking for a new host.

So, I encouraged the living relative to renounce, bind, and cast out the impersonating spirit that appeared in the dream *(since they had been happy to see it, thinking it was their deceased relative)*. Also, I instructed them to break any unholy covenants made with it. Refer to the *"Prayer After Dreams About the Deceased."*

Prayer After Dreams About the Deceased

~~~

Pray this after having a dream that includes deceased relatives, friends, or acquaintances.

Dear Lord,

Be exalted above the heavens, and Your glory above all the earth; That Your beloved may be delivered, save with Your right hand and hear me. Psalm 108:5-6 NKJV

Lord, I repent for my sins and ask for Your mercy and forgiveness.

In the name of Jesus Christ, I bind and send to the abyss every familiar, ancestral, and demonic spirit appearing in any of my dreams.

I cancel and revoke all legal access I may have given to demonic spirits in my dreams. I do not accept those spirits. **I break and cancel all unholy covenants and agreements I may have entered into knowingly or unknowingly, while awake or asleep.** *(Repeat 2x)*

I renounce my acceptance and involvement, in any way and in any form, with the occult—that includes witchcraft, sorcery, divination, tarot cards, secret societies, false religions, demonic games, and idol worship. I close all open doors and portals to the enemy.

I repent for any sins or hostilities toward God by me or my ancestors that may have provided legal entry to my bloodline. I pray for God's mercy and salvation.

In Jesus' name, I pray. Amen.

Psalm 108:5-6, Leviticus 26:40

Note: In addition to the above prayer, you may also want to pray the "Prayer to Break Generational Curses."

Understanding Erotic Dreams

~~~

They look like human beings!

A demon appearing in male form *(incubus),* or in female form *(succubus)* may show up in your dreams to have sexual intercourse. Let's call them erotic demons. Erotic demons tend to show up in dreams before or during a major life transition *(but may also appear at any time to secure a covenant and gain legal access to upset your life).*

You may be in the process of closing a deal, a contract, an offer, a settlement, or about to receive a blessing or breakthrough when they appear. Demons are spiritual beings, and they can see heavenly agents in the spirit realm aligning to deliver your blessings—blessings that they want to stop.

The end goal of erotic demons is to:

- Block your blessings, breakthroughs, success, upward mobility, and forward progress.
- Trick you into an unholy covenant to gain legal entry into your life to steal, kill, and destroy you and your God-ordained purpose and destiny, among other things.

Erotic demons may be drawn to you as a result of:

- Blessings, rewards, or breakthroughs coming your way
- Pornography, lust, masturbation
- Lasciviousness *(i.e., lewd sexual fantasies)*
- Participation in occult activities, past or present
- Spiritual spouse *(a demon claiming to be your husband or wife)*
- Ancestral spirits *(i.e., demons moving through your bloodline)*
- Witchcraft, spells, hexes, demonic altars, or other occult rituals targeting you

If you had intercourse with the demon in your dream, you should immediately do these four things:

1. **Repent and ask the Lord to help you.**
2. **Renounce your involvement with the demon.**
3. **Break the unholy covenant formed by the sexual encounter.**
4. **Forgive yourself—don't beat yourself up.**

Pray the *"Prayer After an Erotic Dream"* three or more times a week, for at least two weeks.

Note: If you have an erotic dream and have intercourse in the dream, please act quickly and break the unholy covenant that you were tricked into forming. Do not procrastinate. This will allow the enemy to set up traps and strongholds *(though they can be broken).* Bind the spirit of procrastination, if needed. Break the unholy covenant quickly to block the enemy. Fight for your best life in Christ!

Just a little about marine spirits. Incubus and succubus are often classified as marine spirits. Marine spirits *(demons)* are those from Satan's so-called water kingdom. I give no credence to them. I really don't care where they come from. **They're not special.**

At the end of the day, who really cares where the demons come from anyway? We bind and rebuke them in the same way, and they shudder and scatter at the name of Jesus—no matter if they're from land, air, or water. I wish people would stop calling them out and hyping them. I have fought all kinds and won through Jesus. Our spiritual armor subdues them whether they are wet or dry, and that's all I care to say about them. **They are defeated.**

~~~

BLESS THE LORD JESUS, WHO IS GREATER THAN ALL AND ABOVE ALL! AMEN.

Prayer After an Erotic Dream

~~~

Holy Father,

What a mighty God You are! *You have delivered us from the power of darkness and translated us into the kingdom of Your dear Son, Jesus Christ. (Colossians 1:13)*

Lord, who can compare to You? You are holy and righteous, mighty, and all-powerful. Your love, grace, and mercy have no limits. I am humbled by Your goodness and thankful for Your faithfulness. Please forgive me for my sins.

By the power of Jesus Christ, I bind and send to the abyss all demonic and familiar spirits that were present in any of my dreams.

I repent for and renounce my involvement with erotic demons or familiar spirits who pretended to be human beings in my dreams.

I bind and send to the abyss all enemy forces organized against me.

I break, cancel, and renounce all unholy covenants that I entered into with erotic and unholy spirits in my dreams.

- **I command all spiritual spouses to depart from me. I renounce my involvement with you. I do not want or accept you anymore. I bind you and cast you into the abyss. Release me right now, and do not return. *(Repeat 2x)***

- I bind and send to the abyss all demons under the command of, and including the spirit of sexual impurity that may be attached to me. I do not want you or accept you. Release me right now, and do not return!

- I bind and send to the abyss all demons on assignment to cause me sickness, delays, hindrances, upsets, disappointments, monetary issues, calamities, losses, missed opportunities, accidents, and any other setbacks, or afflictions in my health, finances, spiritual growth, family, *marriage,* job, *business, ministry,* or any other areas of my life.
- I repent for any acts of witchcraft or sorcery committed by my ancestors or me, and I break any unholy covenants affecting me through my bloodline or my own actions.
- I bind and send to the abyss all familiar spirits and demons summoned against me.

(Restore your blessings)

- I pray for all settlements, contracts, business deals, closings, lawsuits, job offers, promotions, raises, partnerships, or other favorable agreements to be finalized in my favor without delay, according to God's will.
- I pray for a closer walk with God and for favor to be upon me *(and my family).*
- I pray for full restoration of all blessings, rewards, promotions, and breakthroughs that have been delayed or withheld from me.
- I proclaim that I shall go forward and not backward.
- I will be above and not beneath.
- I will enjoy peace, joy, success, healthy relationships, *a healthy marriage,* and life more abundantly.

In Jesus' name, I pray. Amen.

Colossians 1:13, John 10:10, Deuteronomy 28:13

How to Defeat Sexual Lust

~~~

Lust is a formidable demonic spirit. Polite prayers won't get the job done when it comes to defeating this one. Lust is a no-holds-barred scrapper! It has to be renounced, resisted, bound, and cast away—and then you may have to do it again and again. You may have to wrestle "lust" down to the ground until it taps out. You can make it release you through prayer. *(See "Prayer against Lust and Masturbation.")* **You can do all things through Christ who strengthens you. (Philippians 4:13)**

The ruling spirit* over lust is sexual impurity. Sexual impurity must be cast out along with the spirit of lust. Be prepared to spend <u>at least</u> two weeks in spiritual warfare praying four or more times each week. Fasting, along with spiritual warfare prayer, may be needed to secure this win.

Then the disciples came to Jesus privately and asked, "Why could we not cast the demon out?" ***Jesus answered, "This kind of demon does not go out except by prayer and fasting."*** *(Matthew 17:19, 21)*

And Jesus rebuked the demon, and it came out of him ... *that very hour. (Matthew 17:18)*

Whenever I cast the demon of lust out of a person, I start by asking the person if they want the demon. Wisely, they always answer "No." Then I ask them to say aloud, **"I renounce the spirits of sexual impurity and lust. I do not want you. Release me!"** With those words, the demon loses its legal access to that person. Lust must go, but since the lust demon is very stubborn, I continue the assault with this command:

"I bind you, spirits of sexual impurity, lust, and any others working with you. I command you to loose *(release)* this person right now in the mighty name of Jesus and go to the abyss!"

After the demons have been cast out, you must take special care to avoid their reentry. Just as a person recovering from alcoholism is encouraged to avoid drinking, so a person recovering from lust is encouraged to avoid masturbation, pornography, and lasciviousness *(obscene, sexual behaviors, desires, or fantasies).* These sins provide open portals to the lust demon and its ruler, sexual impurity, and they will use these openings to reenter your life. Avoidance of all sexual sins is highly encouraged as a follower of Christ.

Protect the Gates

Days, weeks, or months after departure, the spirits of lust and sexual impurity typically try to reenter through sexual imagery, dreams, or other temptations of the senses via social media, television, etc.

It is important to protect the **eye gate** *(what is seen),* **the ear gate** *(what is heard, erotic sounds),* and the **mind gate** *(what is thought—think on Godly things).* Protect your gates *(eyes, ears, and thoughts)* to prevent those demons from getting back into your life.

Know that *God will not tempt you, for God cannot be tempted by evil, nor does He Himself tempt anyone. But each one is tempted when they are drawn away by their own desires and enticed. Then, when desire has conceived, it gives birth to sin, and sin, when it is full-grown, brings forth death. (James 1:13-15)*

If, however, the unclean spirits do return—just pick up your weapons of warfare *(spiritual warfare prayers)* and slay them again.

It's okay to read prayers. People in the occult do it with great effectiveness, but Christians have been deceived into believing that printed prayers are not sincere or effective. Christians have to mature and put away unfruitful, unscriptural narratives that leave them clobbered, beleaguered, and defeated. I have experienced great spiritual triumphs by reading and repeating **printed** spiritual warfare prayers. Reading them makes them no less effective. Instead, it does the opposite. So, read and repeat as often as needed.

Avoid Masturbation

The sin of masturbation elicits sexual fantasies *(lasciviousness)* and/or pornography. Masturbation can become an addiction, and it opens the door to other demonic spirits, including spiritual spouses. Spiritual husbands and wives are very destructive. They want you for themselves and will go to various extremes to drive away your physical spouse or block any potential spouses if you are unmarried. Repent and ask the Lord to help you stop engaging in masturbation.

Break the Covenant

Typically, if a demon has a hold on you, an unholy covenant has been formed. You should break any unholy covenants with sexual impurity, lust, masturbation, and any others to get free. If you do not break the contract/covenant, they will certainly return holding your spiritual contract in hand and demanding access to your mind *(soul)* and body. They will return time and time again until you break the covenant.

Breaking an unholy covenant is as simple as saying, *"I renounce my involvement with sexual impurity, masturbation, lust, spiritual spouses, or demons of any kind, and I break all unholy covenants I have made with them. In Jesus' name. Amen."*

With that, you will remove their legal access to you. You can "shoo" them away, and they will stay away for longer periods of time—or possibly never return—unless you reopen the door. Fight for your best life in Christ!

*Ruling spirit – Demons have ranks. The ruling spirit is the one leading a group of demons. The sexual impurity demon has under its command a host of demons, including (but not limited to) lust, masturbation, homosexuality, bestiality, pedophilia, harlotry, promiscuity, rape, incest, formication, and fragility.

Prayer Against Lust and Masturbation

~~~

Start by avoiding lusty temptations of the eyes, ears, or other senses. Pray this four or more times weekly for at least two weeks or until you get free. This can be a hefty spiritual battle, but you can pray to win.

Father in heaven,

I give You thanks. You sent Your only begotten Son to heal the brokenhearted, to proclaim liberty to the captives, and set at liberty those who are oppressed. (Luke 4:18)

Lord, I want liberty. I want to be free from sexual impurity, *lust, and/or masturbation.*

I acknowledge my sins and ask for Your forgiveness. I plead the blood of Jesus upon myself. Please cleanse me of impure thoughts and desires.

I choose to submit to You, Lord, and I resist the devil. Lead me away from temptations and deliver me from evil. I renounce any covenants I have made with unclean spirits, including sexual spirits and spiritual spouses. Help me to find and follow paths of righteousness and grant me wisdom and strength to avoid entanglement in yokes of bondage.

(Pray against lust)

I reject and resist all spirits of sexual impurity and lust, including spiritual spouses. I do not want or accept any of you. *(Repeat 2x)*

I bind and send to the abyss the spirit of lust and any spirits above or beneath it in rank. I command all unclean spirits to release me now and go into the abyss. I close all entrances and portals that grant demons access to my body, my soul, or any areas of my life. Do not return to me. I will not accept you.

(Pray against masturbation, if needed. If not, skip to "Pray for restoration" below.)

I renounce, resist, and send to the abyss all demons and spirits of sexual impurity that compel me to masturbate, including spiritual spouses. Release me now! I close all entrances and portals that grant unclean spirits access to my body, my soul[1], or any areas of my life. I do not want or accept you. *(Repeat 2x)*

(Pray for restoration)

Lord, please take me under Your wings and teach me Your ways. Reveal to me the shortcomings and sins that hinder or set me back. Give me the strength to reject unclean thoughts[2] that entice me and cause me to sin.

Cleanse me, Lord, and make me whole. Create in me a clean heart and renew a right spirit in me.

Set me on a path to live an abundant, fulfilling life that pleases You and brings glory to Your name.

In Jesus' name, I pray. Amen.

Luke 4:18, Galatians 5:1, James 1:5, James 1:14-15, James 4:7, Psalm 51:10, John 10:10

[1] The soul/mind is where decisions are made.
[2] You can resist unclean thoughts by simply saying, "I reject these thoughts. Get away from me, unclean spirits."

Protection Prayers

~~~

Do not be afraid nor dismayed for the battle is not yours, but God's.
2 Chronicles 20:15

~~~

Remember, God is with you and
He wants you to win every spiritual battle.

The Holy Spirit woke me up one morning around 5 a.m. This was not unusual. However, before I could fully open my eyes, He told me to break witchcraft off one of my relatives—let's call them Alex. He told me to break witchcraft off Alex's vehicle, too. The situation had to be serious for a 5 a.m. battle. I did as the Lord instructed and went to war!

Later that morning, I contacted Alex to ask what was going on. Alex could not talk but stopped by my home after work to chat. Alex looked unusually tired and confirmed the Holy Spirit was correct. Apparently, Alex had rejected the advances of a co-worker who was known to be involved in the occult, and she had decided to "fix" Alex.

When an occult worker decides to **"fix"** someone, that typically implies that they are going to use unholy tactics, such as witchcraft, voodoo, or sorcery to harm or control them.

So, Alex, a Christian, was under demonic attack. Alex endured a variety of upsets, losses, sleepless nights, and troubles. Alex was doing the right thing by fighting back and binding demons. Nevertheless, there was no peace for Alex, and troubles were closing in from all sides. Alex became drained and exhausted. Alex needed help.

It was on! The warfare that began at 5 a.m. that morning went on for days, and in less than a week, things had turned around for Alex. All of the spells, incantations, demonic altars, curses, and hexes were broken, and Alex was flourishing again.

In the end, Alex won! Alex was promoted to a much higher position in another company. I understand that the occult worker was later demoted, but we did not pray evil upon her. Vengeance is the Lord's. He will repay. Instead, we prayed for her to be saved and to turn away from wickedness. Prayerfully, she has or will come to Jesus.

The following pages contain protection prayers like the one used at 5 a.m. one morning and for many days thereafter to block and stop a witchcraft attack.

If you suspect that someone is working witchcraft on you or has hired someone to do it, use the prayers in this section *(one or all of them)* to stop the attacks. Commit to praying for three or more days a week for two weeks.

Open your mouth, use your God-given authority, and pray to win!

Protection from Witchcraft and Evil

~~~

Father, in the name of Jesus,

I will call upon You, for You are worthy to be praised. I will lift up my voice to You and be saved from all my enemies. (From Psalm 18:3)

I repent for my sins and ask for Your forgiveness. I also choose to forgive others. Please help me.

I plead the blood of Jesus upon myself, and I proclaim that no weapons formed against me shall prosper.

By the power of Jesus Christ, I cancel and nullify any negative words, spells, and curses spoken against me.

I bind and send to the abyss all demonic and familiar spirits summoned to carry out and enforce any negative words, spells, and curses spoken against me. *(Repeat 2x)*

I revoke all forms of witchcraft, sorcery, and divination aimed at me.

Let every occult device being used to mirror my face or look into my future become faulty, broken, destroyed, and stop working.

Confound the diviners, Lord, according to Your word.

Let those who astral project into my space find their cords cut so they will retreat and repent.

- I bind and send to the abyss every demonic and familiar spirit connected to magic mirrors, demonic altars, or other occult objects serving as sources of power to watch me, monitor me, hinder me, curse me, steal, kill, or destroy me by any means and in any areas of my life.

- Let all forms of the occult fail that use my name, image, possessions, or any parts of my DNA *(e.g., hair, nails, etc.)* to harm me or summon evil forces against me.

- I bind and send to the abyss every demonic power invoked to enforce evil enchantments, demonic altars, ritual sacrifices, and other forms of witchcraft, sorcery, divination, and occult practices against me, or *my family, my marriage, my children,* my health, income, residence, transportation, possessions, peace, joy, appearance, relationships, progress, success, goals, destiny, or anything else that may negatively affect my life, livelihood, survival, or reputation.

I banish any demons that are negatively affecting me at work because of inconspicuous witches or sorcerers in positions of authority over me.

I bind and send to the abyss any demon, familiar spirit, serpent, and ancestral spirit that has been summoned to cause me hurt, harm, danger, accidents, confusion, discouragement, depression, attacks on my mind, loss of memory, loss of focus, loss of energy, loss of friends, meaningful relationships, love, or favor.

I bind and send into the abyss all mind-blocking, destiny-impeding demons that distract me, or keep me from doing my own will and the will of God.

I ask the Lord to overthrow all strongmen[1] in heavenly realms that are standing against me or hindering my progress, success, blessings, rewards, opportunities, breakthroughs, or spiritual growth.

I command the east winds, and forces of destruction, calamity, loss, famine, lack, hardship, stagnation, sickness, disease, death, and poverty to turn away from me. *(Exodus 10:13)*

I pray for restoration, deliverance, and pleasant fruits to blow into my life. *(Exodus 10:19, Song of Solomon 4:16)*

Let my enemies be confounded, repented, defeated, and retreated. May they turn away from evil and turn to Jesus!

I renounce and break all unholy covenants and agreements that I may have entered knowingly or unknowingly, while awake or asleep.

(Blessings)

I proclaim that I shall go forward and not backward. I shall succeed and not fail. I shall be the head and not the tail—above and not beneath.

I reclaim all blessings, promotions, opportunities, and virtues lost to spiritual thieves and command them all to be returned now, in Jesus' name.

I pray for the accelerated manifestation of my blessings and rewards in these latter days.

I pray that my gifts and talents will be realized, maximized, and used for God's glory and for the benefit and blessing of others.

I pray for more wisdom, love, faith, and understanding so that I may remain strong in the Lord during these perilous times.

In Jesus' name, I pray. Amen.

[1] *Strongmen = Rulers, powers, authorities, principalities, spiritual wickedness in heavenly (or high) places (Ephesians 6:12)*

Isaiah 54:17, Isaiah 44:25, Exodus 10:13, Exodus 10:19, Deuteronomy 28:13, Proverbs 4:7, Micah 3:7

Family Protection from Witchcraft and Evil

~~~

Father in heaven,

Your way is perfect, and Your word is tested and proven. You are a shield to all who trust in You. (Psalm 18:30)

I repent for my sins and ask for forgiveness. I also remit the sins of *(enter names)*. I lift us up in prayer together.

By the power of Jesus Christ, I cancel and revoke any negative words, spells, and curses spoken against us and all forms of witchcraft, sorcery, and divination targeting us.

I bind and send to the abyss all demonic and familiar spirits summoned to execute negative words, spells, and curses spoken against us.

I proclaim that no weapons formed against us shall prosper.

Let every occult device being used to mirror our faces or look into our futures become faulty, broken, destroyed, and stop working. Let the diviners be confounded, and let us be cloaked in the spirit so enemy forces cannot locate us with occult devices.

- I bind and send to the abyss every demonic and familiar spirit connected to magic mirrors, demonic altars, or other occult objects serving as sources of power to watch us, monitor us, hinder us, curse us, steal, kill, or destroy us by any means and in any areas of our lives.

- I close all open doors to the lives and circumstances of each person named in this prayer.

- Let all forms of the occult fail that use our names, images, possessions, or any parts of our DNA *(e.g., hair, nails)* to harm us or summon evil forces against us.

- I bind and send to the abyss every demonic power summoned to enforce evil enchantments, demonic altars, ritual sacrifices, and other forms of witchcraft, sorcery, divination, and occult practices against us, or *our families, marriages, children,* health, income, residences, transportation, relationships, possessions, peace, joy, appearance, progress, success, destinies, or anything else that may negatively affect our lives, livelihoods, survival, or reputations.

I banish any demons that are negatively affecting us at work because of inconspicuous witches or sorcerers in positions of authority over us.

I bind and send to the abyss any demon, familiar spirit, serpent, and ancestral spirit that has been summoned and sent to cause us hurt, harm, accidents, confusion, discouragement, depression, attacks on the mind, loss of memory, loss of focus, loss of energy, loss of friends, meaningful relationships, love, or favor.

I bind and send to the abyss all mind-blocking, destiny-impeding demons that distract us, or keep us from doing our own will and the will of God.

I ask the Lord to overthrow all strongmen[1] in the heavens that are standing against us or hindering our progress, success, blessings, rewards, opportunities, breakthroughs, or spiritual growth.

I command the east winds, and forces of destruction, calamity, loss, famine, lack, hardship, stagnation, sickness, disease, death, and poverty to turn away from us. *(Exodus 10:13)*

I pray for restoration, deliverance, and pleasant fruits to blow into each of our lives. *(Exodus 10:19, Song of Solomon 4:16)*

Let our enemies be confounded, repented, defeated, and retreated. May they turn away from evil and turn to Jesus!

(Blessings)

I proclaim that we each shall go forward and not backward. We shall succeed and not fail. We shall be the heads and not the tails—above and not beneath.

I pray for the restoration of all blessings, promotions, and any virtues we have lost to spiritual thieves. I command them all to be returned to us now, in Jesus' name.

I pray for the accelerated manifestation of our blessings and rewards in these latter days.

I pray that our gifts and talents will be realized, maximized, and used for God's glory and for the benefit and blessing of others.

I pray that we shall prosper in health, wealth, and in all things, even as our souls prosper.

I pray that we will be strong in our faith in the Lord during these perilous times and continue to grow in wisdom, love, faith, and righteousness.

In Jesus' name, I pray. Amen.

[1] *Strongmen = Rulers, powers, authorities, principalities, spiritual wickedness in heavenly (or high) places (Ephesians 6:12)*

Psalm 18:30, John 20:23, Isaiah 54:17, Isaiah 44:25, Exodus 10:13 & 19, Deuteronomy 28:13, 3 John 1:2, Song of Solomon 4:16

Psalm 64 Protection Prayer

~~~

This prayer contains excerpts from Psalm 64, a psalm of David. It was a petition to God to protect his life from enemy oppression. It is still as powerful and effective today as it was in King David's time.

Holy and righteous Father,

There is none like You! Let the whole earth shout joyfully to You, God! Let us lift up our voices and sing about the glory of Your name and make Your praise glorious! (From Psalm 66:1-2)

I call upon You, my God, and my Protector.

I repent for my sins and ask for Your forgiveness.

I pray for Your protection over my life and all that pertains to me.

You, Lord, are my salvation and hope. Your thoughts toward me are always good.

You have seen the vengeance, jealousy, hatred, and schemes against me. Those who oppose me aim bitter words, like arrows, and shoot them at me. They do not fear. They do not love. They do not forgive. They have no mercy or consideration for my life or livelihood.

They encourage themselves with evil plans for me. They talk of hiding snares and say, *"Who will see it?"*

Deliver me and protect my life. Hide me from the threats of the enemy and help me to forgive those who seek my harm. Vengeance belongs to You.

You will turn their own tongues and evil plans against them, for no weapons formed against me shall prosper.

I bind and send to the abyss all demons sent to discourage me, entrap me, confuse me, hinder me, or block my blessings, my breakthroughs, or advancement. *(Repeat 2x)*

I bind and send to the abyss all demons sent to wreak havoc in my life and attack my health, wealth, income, livelihood, *family, marriage, children,* destiny, mental faculties, possessions, *ministry, education,* peace, safety, freedom, and overall well-being.

I bind and send to the abyss all demonic forces sent to carry out curses, covenants, hexes, spells, witchcraft, sorcery, voodoo candles, or other evil enchantments against me. I command all attacks against me to stop right now, in the mighty name of Jesus!

I bind, cancel, and stop any attacks that are directed toward me from the enemy and the avenger.

I uproot and burn all ungodly tares that I have sown.

I pray for Your help, Lord, to grow and overcome all that causes me to slip and fall. Give me strength and power over all that besets me and weighs me down. In You, Lord, I am victorious!

I pray that I shall prosper in all things and be in good health, even as my soul prospers. Let peace, joy, and order manifest in my life now.

I bless those who pray for my well-being. I pray that they are always safe, growing in prosperity, and abounding in good health.

I pray to receive favor from all who I encounter upon the earth throughout my life.

Protect me, Lord, from deadly assaults, mass shootings, hurt, harm, danger, terror, and threats of any kind.

In Jesus' name, I pray. Amen.

Jeremiah 29:11, Psalm 64:1-3, Psalm 64:5, Psalm 64:8-9, Lamentations 3:59-61, Psalm 118:17, 3 John 1:2

Psalm 64 Protection for Family and Others

~~~

Father in heaven, You are holy and righteous!

There is none like You! Let the whole earth shout joyfully to You, God! Let us lift up our voices and sing about the glory of Your name and make Your praise glorious! (From Psalm 66:1-2)

I repent for my sins and ask for Your forgiveness.

I lift up *(names)* and myself in prayer. I plead the blood of Jesus and put up a hedge of protection around us all. I pray for Your protection over our lives and over all our affairs.

Lord, You have seen the plans and schemes of those who are against us… Plans to do us harm and not good.

- They aim bitter words, like arrows, and shoot them at us.
- They do not fear. They do not love. They do not forgive. They have no mercy or consideration for our lives or livelihoods.
- Preserve us, Lord. Protect us and hide us from the secret plots of those who are our enemies.
- You will turn their own tongues and evil plans against them.

I proclaim that no weapons formed against us shall prosper and that we shall not die but live and declare the works of the Lord.

I bind and send to the abyss all demons sent to discourage us, confuse us, hinder us, or block our blessings and success.

I bind and cancel the assignments of all demons sent to wreak havoc in our lives or attack the health, wealth, income, destiny, future, *marriage, children,* mental faculties, belongings, *education,* peace, safety, freedom, and overall well-being of any person named in this prayer.

I bind and send to the abyss all demonic forces sent to carry out curses, covenants, hexes, spells, witchcraft, sorcery, voodoo candles, or other evil enchantments against us. I command all attacks against us to stop right now, in the mighty name of Jesus!

I bind, cancel, and stop any attacks that are directed toward any of us from the enemy and the avenger.

I bless those who bless us and pray that they are always safe, growing in prosperity, and abounding in good health.

I pray that we shall prosper in all things and be in good health, even as our souls prosper.

I pray for peace, joy, order, comfort, and blessings to manifest into our lives.

I pray for each of us to receive favor from all whom we encounter on the earth.

I pray for the Lord to protect us all from deadly assaults, mass shootings, hurt, harm, danger, terror, and threats of any kind.

Lord, have mercy on us all. Let Your kingdom come, and Your will be done in our lives.

In Jesus' name, I pray. Amen.

Psalm 64:1-3, Lamentations 3:59-61, Psalm 118:17, Luke 6:28, 3 John 1:2, Matthew 6:10

Isaiah 41 Covering Prayer

~~~

(Cover yourself often with these powerful words from Isaiah 41:10-13.)

Father in heaven,

I repent for my sins and ask You to forgive me.

Unto thee, O Lord, do I lift up my soul. O my God, I trust in Thee. Let me not be ashamed. Let not my enemies triumph over me. (Psalm 25:2)

I will not fear nor be dismayed; for You are with me. You are my God. You will strengthen me; yes, You will help me and uphold me with the right hand of Your righteousness.

According to Your word, all who were incensed against me shall be ashamed and confounded. They shall be as nothing; and they that strive with me shall perish. I shall seek them, and not find them, even them that contended with me.

They that war against me shall be as nothing at all. For the Lord my God, will hold my right hand, saying unto me, *"Fear not; I will help you."*

Thanks be unto God, who always causes me *(and my family)* to triumph in Christ.

In Jesus' name, I pray. Amen.

Psalm 25:2, Isaiah 41:10-13, 2 Corinthians 2:14

The Lord's Prayer

~~~

The Lord's Prayer is a gift to us directly from the Lord Jesus Christ. It is the perfect prayer and the model for the prayers in this book. It is short and simple, yet it is the **greatest prayer of all time!** No prayer in this book is greater. This book of prayers would not be complete without it. *Thank You for this gift, Lord Jesus!*

Our Father, which art in heaven,

Hallowed be Thy name.
Thy kingdom come,
Thy will be done on earth,
as it is in heaven.

Give us this day our daily bread.
And forgive us our trespasses, as we forgive those who trespass against us.[1]

And lead us not into temptation, but deliver us from evil:
For Thine is the kingdom, and the power, and the glory, forever.
Amen.

Matthew 6:9-13

[1]*Or you may say, "And forgive us our debts as we forgive our debtors."*

Workplace Prayers

~~~

The prayers on the following pages are provided to cover you in the workplace.

Many years ago, my manager at work asked me to provide her with information about my coworkers. My coworkers were of varying races, genders, and sexual preferences, and they were known to confide in me and seek God's counsel to help with their personal matters. She knew this and wanted insight into their personal lives. She also wanted to know their true opinions of her.

I'm not a fan of this type of leadership *(if that's what you want to call it)*. More importantly, I could not, with a good conscience, betray the confidence and trust of my colleagues. The whole thing was wrong on many levels, and I knew the Lord would not be pleased, either.

Often in life, we are faced with situations that essentially challenge us to make a choice to please God or please mankind. Our choice should always be to **please God.**

So, I respectfully refused to betray my colleagues. Months later, I was unemployed with $2,000/month in rent, three car notes, two sons in college, a daughter involved in high school activities, and many other expenses. However, God's grace covered my family and me during that time, and we experienced **miracles, almost daily,** that sustained us. I felt God's presence in a big way *(Psalm 46:1)*. My faith increased, and I became more humble, thankful, and merciful *(Romans 8:28)*.

Anyway, I found another job and was faced with another ungodly compromise. Within six months, my head was once again on the chopping block. I was unemployed again.

Faithfully, the Lord provided again in miraculous ways. We lost nothing, and all of the bills were paid on time.

After experiencing two layoffs in less than two years, I had to dig deeper. I had to upgrade my spiritual warfare strategies to end that pattern of layoffs. I began to write workplace prayers.

My Sin and Repentance

During that period of unemployment, the Holy Spirit revealed that I had made my job into a small god. He revealed that on many occasions, when I had free time *(after work or on weekends),* I had chosen to perform work duties instead of spending time reading, praying, worshipping, or praising God. He reminded me of times when He would compel me to spend time with Him, and I would not. Shamefully, I chose work instead of the Lord, making the job a false god. Anything that we choose **instead of God** is a false god. I repented.

The Lord forgave me, and I lost nothing during those job transitions. Instead, I gained more spiritual insight and wisdom. So, the third time my head was on the chopping block, I prayed the workplace prayers in this book. I prayed them both every day for two weeks. This layoff pattern had to stop! The enemy was tearing me down inside, and I knew he would continue until I was in tatters. No more! The third time, I won! The enemy retreated, and I kept my job. Enough was enough!

I continued to pray these prayers once every few months just to prevent or minimize any attacks. Also, if things started to feel funny on the job, I'd pull out my prayers and pray them for several days.

Others who were good employees used the prayers after finding themselves in similar situations, with heads on chopping blocks. They, too, survived.

All glory goes to God, Jesus, and the Holy Spirit.

Note: Sometimes, it is God's will for you to move on from one job to another or pursue something else (i.e., ministry, your own business, etc.). If that's not the case, the prayers can help you win against evil, witchcraft, and attacks at work.

Protection Prayer for the Workplace

~~~

Father in heaven,

I proclaim Your power! You are awesome in Your sanctuary. You give power and strength to Your people. All praises be to You, Lord God! (From Psalm 68:34-35)

Lord, I acknowledge my sins and ask You to forgive me. I repent.

If I have committed any offenses, political missteps, or sins in my workplace, please forgive me, shield me, and protect my job.

- Give me time, and mercy to make corrections.
- Give me wisdom, knowledge, and divine insight to improve.
- Help me to perform at a higher level to honor You, Lord God.
- Grant me favor in the workplace with my leadership and peers.
- Help me to forgive those who have hurt or disappointed me at work and compel others to forgive me, as well.

I plead the blood of Jesus upon myself and pray for a hedge of protection at work.

I command all demonic warfare against me at *(enter company name, city, state)* to stop right now, in the name of Jesus! *(Repeat 2x)*

I bind and send to the abyss all demons that have been summoned to attack me on my job or to enforce evil words, evil wishes, evil desires, evil plots, demonic altars, occult sacrifices, spells, charms, hexes, potions, incantations, witchcraft, sorcery, and divination toward my job, *children, spouse, marriage,* relationships, health, wealth, progress, destiny, finances or any other areas of my life.

I ask the Lord to overthrow all rulers, powers, and authorities in the heavens that are blocking or delaying my progress, success, spiritual growth, rewards, blessings, breakthroughs, promotions, opportunities, or any good thing that God wants to bestow upon me.

I ask You, Lord, to intervene and put an end to all enemy attempts to terminate me, humiliate me, hinder me, set me up, set me back, use racism or ageism[1] against me, destroy my confidence, oppress me, suppress me, take advantage of me, and look for my shortcomings to bring me to shame.

I break every curse and block every evil plan or trap devised against me at work. I cast down all demonic enforcers[2] of evil and pray for those who curse or conspire against me to repent.

I bind and send to the abyss all demons and familiar spirits in my workplace that are using people to monitor me, watch me, report on me, work against me, sabotage me, harm me, destroy me, delay my advancement, speak negatively or falsely against me, cause me to be disliked, hated, targeted, bullied, stagnated, frustrated, confused, discouraged, depressed, afflicted, or unmotivated.

Let peace surround me in my workplace.

I pray for the manifestation of raises, promotions, success, and upward mobility in my job, and in my life, according to God's will.

Lord, please lift me up to be victorious, encouraged, enlightened, joyful, satisfied, clear-minded, inspired, and motivated at work.

Let Your lovingkindness and Your truth uphold me, guide me, and strengthen me to remain strong in the faith and walk in love toward all.

In Jesus' name, I pray. Amen.

Psalm 68:34-35 (NIV), Colossians 3:23 (NIV), Ephesians 6:12

[1]*Ageism—Workplace discrimination based on age (especially seniors).*
[2]*Demonic enforcers—Unholy beings that carry out evil deeds resulting from occult activities.*

Prayer Against Job Termination

~~~

*If you have experienced multiple job terminations within a short period—particularly if you have been a good employee—there may be ruling spirits pursuing you from job to job to destroy your reputation, confidence, self-esteem, and ability to earn a living. **Consider praying this add-on to the "Prayer for the Workplace."***

NOTE: Christians with a calling from God on their lives <u>may</u> experience job terminations or subtle threats of termination more than others. Do not be discouraged. Do not become weary in well doing. Stand strong! Fight!

By the authority given to me through Christ Jesus, I put on the whole armor of God and take a stand. I ask God Almighty to overthrow all rulers, powers, and authorities in the heavens that follow and pursue me from one employer to the next to destroy me.

I bind and send to the abyss all demons and familiar spirits warring against me to enforce curses or unholy altars raised against me. I confound, cancel, and revoke all demonic attacks and plans against me at *(enter company name of your employer, city, state)*. I cancel all demonic attacks against my job performance, reputation, peace, and livelihood. I reclaim all my blessings, raises, and promotions. This cycle of terminations or subtle threats of termination stops today!

Dear Lord, I pray that You will avenge me and cause me to recover all that the enemy has blocked, delayed, stolen, or withheld from me. Please give me favor, peace, opportunities, and security in my workplace.

In Jesus' name, I pray. Amen.

Ephesians 6:12

How to Get "Right" With God

~~~

What does it mean to get *"right"* with God?

People often think about getting *"right"* with God when facing troubles, sickness, or death. I had an aunt who was very pleasant and kind. She was an excellent judge of character. No underhanded person could get anything past her, and she would confront them if they tried. She had attended church all her life, but on her deathbed, she looked up at her son and asked, *"How can I be sure I will make it to heaven? How can I be sure I'm 'right' with God?"* Her born-again Christian son led her in a prayer of salvation. Hours later, she passed away. She accepted Jesus in a nick of time. Glory to God! Jesus is the only way to get "right" with God.

> *And just as all people were made sinners because of the disobedience of one man [Adam]; in the same way, they will all be **put right with God** as the result of the obedience of the one man [Christ Jesus]. (Romans 5:19 GNT)*

> *Now that we have been **put right with God** through faith, we have peace with God through our Lord Jesus Christ. (Romans 5:1 GNT)*

According to the Scriptures, there is only one way to get *"right"* *(justified, acceptable, and restored to an upright position)* with God, and that is by accepting The Son of God, Jesus Christ, as Lord and Messiah.

> ***Jesus said, "I am The Way, The Truth, and The Life. No one comes to the Father except through Me." (John 14:6 NKJV)***

> *All the prophets testify about Him, that through His name, everyone who believes in Him [whoever trusts in Jesus, accepting Him as Savior and Messiah] receives forgiveness of sins. Acts 10:43 (AMP)*

Intro to Salvation

~~~

Choose you this day whom you will serve.
Joshua 24:15

If you have not accepted Jesus Christ as your Lord and Savior, please consider doing so now! **The end is near.**

The prayer of salvation is the most important prayer in this book. By praying it, you will become born again *(i.e., your spirit will come alive).* *(See Romans 8:10, 1 Corinthians 15:21-22.)* You will be rescued from the dominion and power of darkness *(Satan's realm).* You will be transferred into The Kingdom of Light *(God's Kingdom)* under the leadership of Jesus Christ, the Messiah and Son of God.

Please know that whoever you choose to follow on earth, whether Jesus or Satan, is who you will follow into eternity. Unfollow Satan. FOLLOW JESUS!

Please pray the "Salvation Prayer" today! Don't delay.

~~~

If you prayed the "Salvation Prayer," you are now born again! **Congratulations, and welcome to the winning side of the battle between good and evil! You're on the right team!**

You are under new management! Your leader is Jesus Christ. Learn of Him by reading the Bible and attending a Holy Spirit-led church. Connect with Him and develop your relationship through prayer *(talking to Him from your heart).* Allow the Holy Spirit to renew your mind, transform you, and guide you into all righteousness. Your life will change, and you will grow in peace.

Salvation Prayer

~~~

Jesus said:
Except a man be born again, he cannot see the Kingdom of God.
John 3:3

Dear heavenly Father,

I admit that I'm a sinner and I ask for Your forgiveness.

I want to turn away from a life of sin.

I want to change so that my life brings You glory.

I confess with my mouth, **Jesus is Lord,**

and I believe in my heart that He was raised from the dead.

I accept Jesus Christ as my Lord and Savior and invite Him into my life now.

I thank You, Lord, that I am a new creature in Christ.

I am now born again.

In Jesus' name, I pray. Amen.

Romans 10:9-10

...That if you confess with your mouth the Lord Jesus and believe in your heart that God has raised Him from the dead, you will be saved. For with the heart one believes unto righteousness, and with the mouth confession is made unto salvation.

Choose to Love

~~~

"Teacher, which is the greatest commandment in the Law?"
Jesus replied: *Love the Lord your God with all your heart and
with all your soul and with all your mind. This is the first and greatest
commandment. And the second is like it: Love your neighbor as yourself.*
Matthew 22:36-39 (NIV)

Regarding "love," John said it best when he wrote:

*Beloved, let us love one another, for love is of God, and everyone
who loves is born of God and knows God. He who does not love does not
know God, for **God is love**. In this, the love of God was manifested
toward us, that God has sent His only begotten Son into the world, that
we might live through Him. In this, is love, not that we loved God, but
that He loved us and sent His Son to be the propitiation for our
sins. Beloved, if God so loved us, we also ought to love one another.*

*If we love one another, God abides in us, and His love has been
perfected in us. By this, we know that we abide in Him, and He in us,
because He has given us of His Spirit. And we have seen and testify
that the Father has sent the Son as Savior of the world. Whoever
confesses that Jesus is the Son of God, God abides in him, and he in God.
God is love, and he who abides in love abides in God, and God in him.*

There is no fear in love; but perfect love casts out fear *because fear
involves torment. But he who fears has not been made perfect in
love. We love Him because He first loved us.*

If someone says, "I love God," and hates his brother, he is a liar; *for
he who does not love his brother whom he has seen, how can he love
God whom he has not seen? And this commandment we have from Him:
that he who loves God must love his brother also. (1 John 4:7-21)*

Choose to love.

Choose to Forgive

~~~

For if you forgive men their trespasses, your heavenly Father will also forgive you. But if you do not forgive men their trespasses, neither will your Father forgive your trespasses. Matthew 6:14-15

Forgiveness is a requirement for a follower of Christ. One of the monikers of our faith is that we forgive. In fact, our relationship with Christ is built on forgiveness. We must forgive others to avoid the fate of the unforgiving servant in the parable of Matthew 18:21-35. The parable recounts how a certain king settled accounts with his servants.

In the parable, the unforgiving servant was forgiven for a debt of **ten thousand**; however, he would not forgive a man who owed him a mere **hundred**. In the end, the unforgiving servant was judged as "wicked," and he was sent to the jailers to be tortured.

This parable is applicable today. If God can forgive us for **ten thousand** or more offenses, why can't we forgive others for less?

Forgiveness is a choice. God chose to forgive us. He gave His only begotten Son, Jesus Christ, to make the ultimate sacrifice—His sinless life—for the forgiveness of our sins. Jesus' sacrifice will mean significantly more when we stand before Him on judgment day, having all our sins laid bare in our faces, and He says, "You are forgiven."

We are new creations in Christ. We should move differently than when we lived in darkness. The Holy Spirit is here to help us change, but we must yield to Him. Conforming to Christ is a process, but now we have a choice. Before Christ, we did not have a choice. We were bound to sin by chains, but now, we are free. We are free to choose right or wrong, love or hate, revenge or forgiveness.

Beloved, do not avenge yourselves, but rather give place to [God's] wrath; for it is written, "Vengeance is Mine, I will repay," says the Lord. (Romans 12:19)

Please obey the Lord and forgive. When you choose to forgive someone who has hurt, wronged, or offended you, initially, you may not feel anything, and that's okay. Remember, forgiveness is a choice, not a feeling. However, if you truly mean it, the Holy Spirit will help you to forgive those who offended you.

Remember, Jesus, on the Cross, facing His enemies, said:

"Father, forgive them, for they do not know what they do." (Luke 23:34)

Please obey the Lord and forgive. Do not find yourself giving account for your life and having to explain why you didn't forgive someone who committed one, two, or a hundred offenses against you when God is willing to forgive you of ten thousand or more offenses against Him.

Unforgiveness can block your blessings and breakthroughs. The tormenting spirits connected to unforgiveness can reopen doors and portals that you had previously closed through spiritual warfare. Unforgiveness is also displeasing to God. Therefore, it is worthwhile to regularly ask the Lord to reveal anyone whom you have not forgiven. Once you identify such a person, say, *"Lord, I choose to forgive (name). Please help me to forgive them."* The Lord is faithful to help you overcome unforgiveness and to keep the blessings and breakthroughs flowing in your life. He loves you and wants the best for you.

Choose to forgive.

Check Your Success

~~~

After you have prayed and broken any unholy covenants and curses *(generational or other)*, you should expect to see some positive changes within 90 days. However, if your situation hasn't started to improve by then, it would be wise to check and make sure there are no open doors to the enemy.

Open doors include unforgiveness, unrepented sins, anger at God, involvement in the occult *(psychic readings, demonic games, tarot cards, etc.)*, serving false gods, idolatry, or holding on to objects such as magic *(or healing)* crystals, statues of false gods *(Buddha, etc.),* items used for witchcraft or other occult activities, and any other objects that encourage you to seek an entity or person other than God. Get rid of unholy objects and anything that distracts you or takes priority over God.

Thou shalt have no other gods before me... and make no graven images... Exodus 20:3-4 (KJV)

It may be necessary to separate yourself from those who draw you away from God and cause you to sin. In Matthew 5:30, Jesus taught:

If your right hand causes you to sin, cut it off and cast it from you; for it is more profitable for you that one of your members perish, than for your whole body to be cast into hell.

Pray warfare prayers again and again, as needed. You are in a battle against a very hateful enemy, but you have the advantage because of Jesus *(See Luke 10:19 and 1 John 4:4).* **You're supposed to win!** Do not accept defeat. Fight for your best life in Christ!

Pray, pray, pray to win!

Protect Your Success

As long as there are demons, spiritual warfare will be necessary. From what the Holy Spirit has taught me *(and I earnestly seek His truth),* there is no such thing as a one-and-done prayer that can permanently ward off the enemy. Demonic warfare requires ongoing effort. 1 Peter 5:8 reads:

Be sober, be vigilant; because your adversary the devil walks about like a roaring lion, seeking whom he may devour. (NKJV)

There are millions of restless demons roaming the earth. Their mission is to steal, kill, and destroy *(John 10:10).* They are persistent and may re-attack in the same area where you defeated them, particularly if there are open doors *(e.g., lingering or hidden fears)*—or you haven't crucified the carnal desires that tempt you and draw you into sin.

James 1:13-15 says:

*Remember, when someone wants to do wrong, it is never God who is tempting him [or her], for God never wants to do wrong and never tempts anyone else to do it. Temptation is the pull of man's own evil thoughts and wishes. These **evil thoughts lead to evil actions** and, afterward, to the death penalty from God. (Living Bible)*

... For all these worldly things, these evil desires—the craze for sex (lust of the flesh), the ambition to buy everything that appeals to you (lust of the eyes), and the pride (of life) that comes from wealth and importance—these are not from God. They are from this evil world itself. 1 John 2:16 (Living Bible)

For instance, you may battle and defeat lust by repeating the "Prayer Against Lust and Masturbation," but weeks or months later, you may have to repeat the process, especially if you are open to watching or participating in temptations of the flesh. That's just one example. There are many other sins wherein the flesh has to be crucified, along with unholy desires, habits, actions, and cravings.

Fight for your best life in Christ. Repeat warfare prayers as often as needed. The extra effort will pay off in the end, so you can maintain and protect your success and enjoy peace, joy, and freedom from oppression.

Conclusion

~~~

Believe it or not, humanity wants an encore of Jesus Christ. They want to experience true love—the kind that only Christ can give. They want to experience miracles, healings, and The Kingdom of God on earth. Until Christ's return, we are His encore.

Let us do our best to represent His kingdom, The Kingdom of Light, in our words and our deeds. Let us resist the devil and the ungodly temptations he presents to us. Stand up and fight like the soldier you are. Use spiritual warfare prayers to defeat the enemy and give no place to the devil to re-enter and derail your life.

Fellow Christians, let us strive to walk together, united under the banner of Christ, who is the Head of the Body.

When we have run our race, when we have fought valiantly to advance The Kingdom of God, then let us bow out gracefully, just like our Savior.

May the Lord bless you and keep you. May the Lord make His face shine upon you and be gracious to you. May the Lord turn His face toward you and give you peace. (Numbers 6:24-26)

With Love,
Your fellow laborer and servant in Christ,
Apostle Tracey L. Smith

Scriptures

~~~

1 Corinthians 10:13 NKJV

No temptation has overtaken you except such as is common to man; but God is faithful, who will not allow you to be tempted beyond what you are able, but with the temptation will also make the way of escape ...

1 John 4:4 KJV

Greater is He that is in you, than he that is in the world.

1 Peter 2:9 NKJV

But you are a chosen generation, a royal priesthood, a holy nation, His own special *(peculiar)* people, that you may proclaim the praises of Him who called you out of darkness into His marvelous light.

2 Chronicles 20:15 NIV

Do not be afraid or discouraged ... for the battle is not yours, but God's.

3 John 1:2 NKJV

Beloved, I pray that you may prosper in all things and be in health, just as your soul prospers.

Ephesians 6:11-12, 14-17 NKJV

[11] Put on the whole armor of God, that you may be able to stand against the wiles of the devil. [12] For we do not wrestle against flesh and blood, but against principalities, against powers, against the rulers of the darkness of this age, against spiritual hosts of wickedness in the heavenly places.

[14] Stand therefore, having girded your waist with truth, having put on the breastplate of righteousness, [15] and having shod your feet with the preparation of the gospel of peace; [16] above all, taking the shield of faith with which you will be able to quench all the fiery darts of the wicked one. [17] And take the helmet of salvation, and the sword of the Spirit, which is the word of God.

Hebrews 4:12 KJV

For the word of God is quick, and powerful, and sharper than any two-edged sword, piercing even to the dividing asunder of soul and spirit, and of the joints and marrow, and is a discerner of the thoughts and intents of the heart.

Joshua 24:15 KJV

And if it seem evil unto you to serve the Lord, choose you this day whom ye will serve ... but as for me and my house, we will serve the Lord.

Lamentations 3:22-23 KJV

²² It is of the Lord's mercies that we are not consumed, because His compassions fail not. ²³ They are new every morning: great is Thy faithfulness.

Luke 10:19 NKJV

Behold, I give you the authority to trample on serpents and scorpions, and over all the power of the enemy, and nothing shall by any means hurt you.

Matthew 6:14 NKJV

If you forgive men their trespasses, your heavenly Father will also forgive you.

Matthew 7:12 NIV

... Do to others what you would have them do to you.

Matthew 7:13-14 NIV

¹³ "Enter through the narrow gate. For wide is the gate and broad is the road that leads to destruction, and many enter through it. ¹⁴ But small is the gate and narrow the road that leads to life, and only a few find it.

Psalm 16:5 NET

Lord, You give me stability and prosperity; You make my future secure.

Psalm 46:1 NKJV

God is our refuge and strength, a very present help in trouble.

Psalm 84:11 KJV

For the Lord God is a sun and shield: the Lord will give grace and glory: no good thing will He withhold from them that walk uprightly.

Romans 3:23 KJV

For all have sinned, and come short of the glory of God.

Romans 8:28 NKJV

And we know that all things work together for good to those who love God, to those who are the called according to His purpose.

Author's Biography

~~~

Tracey L. Smith is the daughter of Charles Redding and the late Mrs. Eloise Finney Redding. Ms. Smith is a divorced mother of three children of whom she is very proud: Matthew, Joshua, and Hannah Smith.

Tracey is the eldest of five: Dwayne, Raymond, Semena, and Damon Redding *(from "BeHeard Period"),* respectively.

As a child, Tracey was baptized at Holsey Temple C.M.E. Church *(Atlanta, Georgia).* She also attended Mt. Nebo Baptist Church *(Atlanta (Peoplestown), Georgia).* As an adult, Tracey was a member of and served faithfully at The Living Word Assembly *(Atlanta, Georgia)* and also World Changers Church International *(Atlanta, Georgia).*

Tracey gave her life to Christ in September 1986, two weeks after recovering from a drug overdose in which she died and had a traumatic out-of-body experience. While being pulled down into the dark depths of hell, she cried out to God. He heard her prayer and revived her. All at once, she was back in the hospital room, looking down at her lifeless body. She re-entered her body feet first. The medical staff cheered when she came back to life. Tracey was given a second chance and has been living for Christ ever since.

Her deliverance from drugs was miraculous. The Lord entered her apartment and ministered to her. No rehab was needed. When she got up off the floor after her encounter with the Lord, she was free. She never took another snort of cocaine after that day, though it was offered to her for free. That was in 1986. She received the Holy Spirit with the evidence of speaking in tongues several months later in that same year.

In 1986, Tracey began attending Monday night prayer meetings at The Living Word Assembly Church in Atlanta, where she was a member. That is where she learned about deliverance and spiritual warfare.

In 1987, the Lord called Tracey as an apostle. She had no idea what it meant and initially rejected the call. She had no desire to serve in ministry and be called a "Jezebel." She didn't want to fight with anyone about the calling. She just wanted to pray and serve quietly in the background. So, she kept the calling a secret, hoping it would go away and God would not bring it up again.

Then, one Sunday, she joined the prayer line at church, and the pastor remarked that he saw the words "My apostle" circling Tracey's head. He asked if the Lord had spoken to her about being an apostle. *"Busted!"* She thought to herself. *"God is telling the whole church. I can't hide it anymore."* So, she admitted that the Lord had indeed spoken to her about it, but inside, she was still not accepting it.

Long story short, Tracey eventually accepted her calling—at her mother's graveside. She began accepting speaking engagements in 1989. Tracey was ordained as an apostle and pastor in 1996. She was ordained again in 1997, in a different church. She founded and pastored two churches: The Way of Life Church, and Radiant Light Truth and Learning Center. She also served as the apostle for Teen Church of Houston *(Houston, Texas)*.

Ms. Smith has been engaging in spiritual warfare since 1986 and serving in ministry since 1989. One of her heart's desires is to see the Church unified and mature, and the other is for the Body of Christ to be trained in spiritual warfare to defeat an already-defeated enemy.

Index

~~~

www.ingramcontent.com/pod-product-compliance
Lightning Source LLC
Chambersburg PA
CBHW060413090426

42734CB00011B/2307